STRIFE

A Drama in Three Acts

JOHN GALSWORTHY

With school and acting notes by
JOHN HAMPDEN, M.A.

DUCKWORTH

This impression 1977
First published 1911
Forty-first impression 1960
This Edition 1964
Reprinted 1966 (*twice*), 1967, 1968
Reprinted in larger format 1977

All Rights Reserved

Gerald Duckworth & Co. Ltd.
The Old Piano Factory
43 Gloucester Crescent, London N.W.1

Editorial matter © 1964 by
Gerald Duckworth & Co. Ltd.

ISBN 0 7156 1225 5 (cased)
0 7156 1226 3 (paper)

*All applications respecting amateur performances of
John Galsworthy's plays must be made to*
THE SECRETARY
INCORPORATED SOCIETY OF AUTHORS
84 DRAYTON GARDENS, LONDON, S.W.10

All other applications to the Author's Agents
MESSRS CURTIS BROWN LIMITED
1 CRAVEN HILL
LONDON, W.2
AND 60 E. 56 ST.
NEW YORK 10022
U.S.A.

Printed in Great Britain by
Unwin Brothers Limited
The Gresham Press, Old Woking, Surrey

STRIFE

A Drama in Three Acts

CONTENTS

CHARACTERS OF THE PLAY

JOHN ANTHONY, *Chairman of the Trenartha Tin Plate Works*

EDGAR ANTHONY, *his son* ⎫
FREDERIC H. WILDER ⎪
WILLIAM SCANTLEBURY ⎬ *Directors of the same*
OLIVER WANKLIN ⎭

HENRY TENCH, *Secretary of the same*

FRANCIS UNDERWOOD, C.E., *Manager of the same*

SIMON HARNESS, *a Trade Union official*

DAVID ROBERTS ⎫
JAMES GREEN ⎪
JOHN BULGIN ⎬ *the workmen's committee*
HENRY THOMAS ⎪
GEORGE ROUS ⎭

HENRY ROUS ⎫
LEWIS ⎪
JAGO ⎪
EVANS ⎪ *workmen at the Trenartha Tin*
A BLACKSMITH ⎬ *Plate Works*
DAVIES ⎪
A RED-HAIRED YOUTH ⎪
BROWN ⎭

FROST, *valet to John Anthony*

ENID UNDERWOOD, *wife of Francis Underwood, daughter of John Anthony*

ANNIE ROBERTS, *wife of David Roberts*

Madge Thomas, *daughter of Henry Thomas*
Mrs. Rous, *mother of George and Henry Rous*
Mrs. Bulgin, *wife of John Bulgin*
Mrs. Yeo, *wife of a workman*
A Parlourmaid *to the Underwoods*
Jan, *Madge's brother, a boy of ten*
A Crowd of Men on Strike

The action takes place on February 7th between the hours of noon and six in the afternoon, close to the Trenartha Tin Plate Works, on the borders of England and Wales, where a strike has been in progress throughout the winter.

This play was written in 1907 and first performed in 1909

ACT I

It is noon. In the Underwoods' dining-room a bright fire is burning. On one side of the fireplace are double doors leading to the drawing-room, on the other side a door leading to the hall. In the centre of the room a long dining-table without a cloth is set out as a board table. At the head of it, in the Chairman's seat, sits JOHN ANTHONY, *an old man, big, clean shaven, and high-coloured, with thick white hair, and thick dark eyebrows. His movements are rather slow and feeble, but his eyes are very much alive. There is a glass of water by his side. On his right sits his son* EDGAR, *an earnest-looking man of thirty, reading a newspaper. Next him* WANKLIN, *a man with jutting eyebrows, and silver-streaked light hair, is bending over transfer papers.* TENCH, *the secretary, a short and rather humble, nervous man, with side whiskers, stands helping him. On* WANKLIN'S *right sits* UNDERWOOD, *the Manager, a quiet man, with a long, stiff jaw, and steady eyes. Back to the fire is* SCANTLEBURY, *a very large, pale, sleepy man, with grey hair, rather bald. Between him and the Chairman are two empty chairs.*

WILDER. [*Who is lean, cadaverous, and complaining, with drooping grey moustaches, stands before the fire*] I say, this fire's the devil! Can I have a screen, Tench?

SCANTLEBURY. A screen, ah!

TENCH. Certainly, Mr. Wilder. [*He looks at* UNDERWOOD.] That is—perhaps the Manager—perhaps Mr. Underwood——

SCANTLEBURY. These fireplaces of yours, Underwood——

UNDERWOOD. [*Roused from studying some papers*] A screen? Rather! I'm sorry. [*He goes to the door with a little smile.*]

We're not accustomed to complaints of too much fire down here just now.   [*He speaks as though he holds a pipe between his teeth, slowly, ironically.*

WILDER.   [*In an injured voice*] You mean the men.   H'm!

[UNDERWOOD *goes out.*

SCANTLEBURY.   Poor devils!

WILDER.   It's their own fault, Scantlebury.

EDGAR.   [*Holding out his paper*] There's great distress amongst them, according to the *Trenartha News*.

WILDER.   Oh, that rag!   Give it to Wanklin.   Suit his Radical views.   They call us monsters, I suppose.   The editor of that rubbish ought to be shot.

EDGAR.   [*Reading*] "If the Board of worthy gentlemen who control the Trenartha Tin Plate Works from their arm-chairs in London, would condescend to come and see for themselves the conditions prevailing amongst their workpeople during this strike——"

WILDER.   Well, we *have* come.

EDGAR.   [*Continuing*] "We cannot believe that even their leg-of-mutton hearts would remain untouched."

[WANKLIN *takes the paper from him.*

WILDER.   Ruffian!   I remember that fellow when he hadn't a penny to his name; little snivel of a chap that's made his way by blackguarding everybody who takes a different view to himself.   [ANTHONY *says something that is not heard.*

WILDER.   What does your father say?

EDGAR.   He says "The kettle and the pot."

WILDER.   H'm!   [*He sits down next to* SCANTLEBURY.

SCANTLEBURY.   [*Blowing out his cheeks*] I shall boil if I don't get that screen.

[UNDERWOOD *and* ENID *enter with a screen, which they place before the fire.*   ENID *is tall; she has a small, decided face, and is twenty-eight years old.*

ENID.   Put it closer, Frank.   Will that do, Mr. Wilder? It's the highest we've got.

WILDER.   Thanks, capitally.

SCANTLEBURY. [*Turning, with a sigh of pleasure*] Ah! Merci, Madame!

ENID. Is there anything else you want, father? [ANTHONY *shakes his head.*] Edgar—anything?

EDGAR. You might give me a "J" nib, old girl.

ENID. There are some down there by Mr. Scantlebury.

SCANTLEBURY. [*Handing a little box of nibs*] Ah! your brother uses "J's." What does the manager use? [*With expansive politeness.*] What does your husband use, Mrs. Underwood?

UNDERWOOD. A quill!

SCANTLEBURY. The homely product of the goose.

[*He holds out quills.*

UNDERWOOD. [*Dryly*] Thanks, if you can spare me one. [*He takes a quill.*] What about lunch, Enid?

ENID. [*Stopping at the double doors and looking back*] We're going to have lunch here, in the drawing-room, so you needn't hurry with your meeting.

[WANKLIN *and* WILDER *bow, and she goes out.*

SCANTLEBURY. [*Rousing himself, suddenly*] Ah! Lunch! That hotel—— Dreadful! Did you try the whitebait last night? Fried fat!

WILDER. Past twelve! Aren't you going to read the minutes, Tench?

TENCH. [*Looking for the* CHAIRMAN's *assent, reads in a rapid and monotonous voice*] "At a Board Meeting held the 31st of January at the Company's Offices, 512, Cannon Street, E.C. Present—Mr. Anthony in the chair, Messrs. F. H. Wilder, William Scantlebury, Oliver Wanklin, and Edgar Anthony. Read letters from the Manager dated January 20th, 23rd, 25th, 28th, relative to the strike at the Company's Works. Read letters to the Manager of January 21st, 24th, 26th, 29th. Read letter from Mr. Simon Harness, of the Central Union, asking for an interview with the Board. Read letter from the Men's Committee, signed David Roberts, James Green, John Bulgin, Henry Thomas, George Rous, desiring conference with the

Board; and it was resolved that a special Board Meeting be
called for February 7th at the house of the Manager, for the
purpose of discussing the situation with Mr. Simon Harness and
the Men's Committee on the spot.   Passed twelve transfers,
signed and sealed nine certificates and one balance certificate."
                    [*He pushes the book over to the* CHAIRMAN.
ANTHONY.   [*With a heavy sigh*] If it's your pleasure, sign
the same.   [*He signs, moving the pen with difficulty.*
WANKLIN.   What the Union's game, Tench?   They
haven't made up their split with the men.   What does Harness
want this interview for?
TENCH.   Hoping we shall come to a compromise, I think,
sir; he's having a meeting with the men this afternoon.
WILDER.   Harness!   Ah!   He's one of those cold-blooded,
cool-headed chaps.   I distrust them.   I don't know that we
didn't make a mistake to come down.   What time'll the men
be here?
UNDERWOOD.   Any time now.
WILDER.   Well, if we're not ready, they'll have to wait—
won't do 'em any harm to cool their heels a bit.
SCANTLEBURY.   [*Slowly*] Poor devils!   It's snowing.   *What*
weather!
UNDERWOOD.   [*With meaning slowness*] This house'll be
the warmest place they've been in this winter.
WILDER.   Well, I hope we're going to settle this business in
time for me to catch the 6.30.   I've got to take my wife to
Spain to-morrow.   [*Chattily.*]   My old father had a strike at
his works in '69; just such a February as this.   They wanted
to shoot him.
WANKLIN.   What!   In the close season?
WILDER.   By George, there was no close season for
employers then!   He used to go down to his office with a
pistol in his pocket.
SCANTLEBURY.   [*Faintly alarmed*] Not seriously?
WILDER.   [*With finality*] Ended in his shootin' one of 'em
in the legs.

SCANTLEBURY. [*Unavoidably feeling his thigh*] No? God bless me!

ANTHONY. [*Lifting the agenda paper*] To consider the policy of the Board in relation to the strike. [*There is a silence.*

WILDER. It's this infernal three-cornered duel—the Union, the men, and ourselves.

WANKLIN. We needn't consider the Union.

WILDER. It's my experience that you've always got to consider the Union, confound them! If the Union were going to withdraw their support from the men, as they've done, why did they ever allow them to strike at all?

EDGAR. We've had that over a dozen times.

WILDER. Well, I've never understood it! It's beyond me. They talk of the engineers' and furnacemen's demands being excessive—so they are—but that's not enough to make the Union withdraw their support. What's behind it?

UNDERWOOD. Fear of strikes at Harper's and Tinewell's.

WILDER. [*With triumph*] Afraid of other strikes—now, that's a reason! Why couldn't we have been told that before?

UNDERWOOD. You were.

TENCH. You were absent from the Board that day, sir.

SCANTLEBURY. The men must have seen they had no chance when the Union gave them up. It's madness.

UNDERWOOD. It's Roberts!

WILDER. Just our luck, the men finding a fanatical fire-brand like Roberts for leader. [*A pause.*

WANKLIN. [*Looking at* ANTHONY] Well?

WILDER. [*Breaking in fussily*] It's a regular mess. I don't like the position we're in; I don't like it; I've said so for a long time. [*Looking at* WANKLIN.] When Wanklin and I came down here before Christmas it looked as if the men must collapse. You thought so too, Underwood.

UNDERWOOD. Yes.

WILDER. Well, they haven't! Here we are, going from bad to worse—losing our customers—shares going down!

SCANTLEBURY. [*Shaking his head*] M'm! M'm!

WANKLIN.   What loss have we made by this strike, Tench?

TENCH.   Over fifty thousand, sir!

SCANTLEBURY.   [*Pained*] You don't say!

WILDER.   We shall never get it back.

TENCH.   No, sir.

WILDER.   Who'd have supposed the men were going to stick out like this—nobody suggested that.

[*Looking angrily at* TENCH.

SCANTLEBURY.   [*Shaking his head*] I've never liked a fight—never shall.

ANTHONY.   No surrender!   [*All look at him.*

WILDER.   Who wants to surrender?   [ANTHONY *looks at him.*]   I—I want to act reasonably.   When the men sent Roberts up to the Board in December—then was the time. We ought to have humoured him; instead of that, the Chairman —[*Dropping his eyes before* ANTHONY'S]—er—we snapped his head off.   We could have got them in then by a little tact.

ANTHONY.   No compromise!

WILDER.   There we are!   This strike's been going on now since October, and as far as I can see it may last another six months.   Pretty mess we shall be in by then.   The only comfort is, the men'll be in a worse!

EDGAR.   [*To* UNDERWOOD] What sort of state are they really in, Frank?

UNDERWOOD.   [*Without expression*] Damnable!

WILDER.   Well, who on earth would have thought they'd have held on like this without support!

UNDERWOOD.   Those who know them.

WILDER.   I defy anyone to know them!   And what about tin?   Price going up daily.   When we do get started we shall have to work off our contracts at the top of the market.

WANKLIN.   What do you say to that, Chairman?

ANTHONY.   Can't be helped!

WILDER.   Shan't pay a dividend till goodness knows when!

SCANTLEBURY.   [*With emphasis*] We ought to think of the

shareholders. [*Turning heavily.*] Chairman, I say we ought to think of the shareholders. [ANTHONY *mutters.*

SCANTLEBURY. What's that?

TENCH. The Chairman says he *is* thinking of you, sir.

SCANTLEBURY. [*Sinking back into torpor*] Cynic!

WILDER. It's past a joke. *I* don't want to go without a dividend for years if the Chairman does. We can't go on playing ducks and drakes with the Company's prosperity.

EDGAR. [*Rather ashamedly*] I think we ought to consider the men. [*All but* ANTHONY *fidget in their seats.*

SCANTLEBURY. [*With a sigh*] We mustn't think of our private feelings, young man. That'll never do.

EDGAR. [*Ironically*] I'm not thinking of our feelings. I'm thinking of the men's.

WILDER. As to that—we're men of business.

WANKLIN. That *is* the little trouble.

EDGAR. There's no necessity for pushing things so far in the face of all this suffering—it's—it's cruel.

[*No one speaks, as though* EDGAR *had uncovered something whose existence no man prizing his self-respect could afford to recognize.*

WANKLIN. [*With an ironical smile*] I'm afraid we mustn't base our policy on luxuries like sentiment.

EDGAR. I detest this state of things.

ANTHONY. We didn't seek the quarrel.

EDGAR. I know that, sir, but surely we've gone far enough.

ANTHONY. No. [*All look at one another.*

WANKLIN. Luxuries apart, Chairman, we must look out what we're doing.

ANTHONY. Give way to the men once and there'll be no end to it.

WANKLIN. I quite agree, but—— [ANTHONY *shakes his head.*] You make it a question of bedrock principle? [ANTHONY *nods.*] Luxuries again, Chairman! The shares are below par.

WILDER. Yes, and they'll drop to a half when we pass the next dividend.

SCANTLEBURY.   [*With alarm*] Come, come!   Not so bad as that.

WILDER.   [*Grimly*] You'll see!   [*Craning forward to catch* ANTHONY's *speech.*]   I didn't catch——

TENCH.   [*Hesitating*] The Chairman says, sir, "Fais que—que—devra——"

EDGAR.   [*Sharply*] My father says: "Do what we ought—and let things rip."

WILDER.   Tcha!

SCANTLEBURY.   [*Throwing up his hands*] The Chairman's a Stoic—I always said the Chairman was a Stoic.

WILDER.   Much good that'll do us.

WANKLIN.   [*Suavely*] Seriously, Chairman, are you going to let the ship sink under you, for the sake of—a principle?

ANTHONY.   She won't sink.

SCANTLEBURY.   [*With alarm*] Not while I'm on the Board I hope.

ANTHONY.   [*With a twinkle*] Better rat, Scantlebury.

SCANTLEBURY.   What a man!

ANTHONY.   I've always fought them; I've never been beaten yet.

WANKLIN.   We're with you in theory, Chairman.   But we're not all made of cast-iron.

ANTHONY.   We've only to hold on.

WILDER.   [*Rising and going to the fire*] And go to the devil as fast as we can!

ANTHONY.   Better go to the devil than give in!

WILDER.   [*Fretfully*] That may suit you, sir, but it doesn't suit me, or anyone else I should think.

[ANTHONY *looks him in the face—a silence.*

EDGAR.   I don't see how we can get over it that to go on like this means starvation to the men's wives and families.

[WILDER *turns abruptly to the fire, and* SCANTLEBURY *puts out a hand to push the idea away.*

WANKLIN.   I'm afraid again that sounds a little sentimental.

EDGAR.   Men of business are excused from decency, you think?

WILDER. Nobody's more sorry for the men than I am, but if they [*lashing himself*] choose to be such a pig-headed lot, it's nothing to do with us; we've quite enough on *our* hands to think of ourselves and the shareholders.

EDGAR. [*Irritably*] It won't kill the shareholders to miss a dividend or two; I don't see that *that's* reason enough for knuckling under.

SCANTLEBURY. [*With grave discomfort*] You talk very lightly of your dividends, young man; I don't know where we are.

WILDER. There's only one sound way of looking at it. We can't go on ruining *ourselves* with this strike.

ANTHONY. No caving in!

SCANTLEBURY. [*With a gesture of despair*] Look at him!

[ANTHONY *is leaning back in his chair. They do look at him.*

WILDER. [*Returning to his seat*] Well, all I can say is, if that's the Chairman's view, I don't know what we've come down here for.

ANTHONY. To tell the men that we've got nothing for them—— [*Grimly.*] They won't believe it till they hear it spoken in plain English.

WILDER. H'm! Shouldn't be a bit surprised if that brute Roberts hadn't got us down here with the very same idea. I hate a man with a grievance.

EDGAR. [*Resentfully*] We didn't pay him enough for his discovery. I always said that at the time.

WILDER. We paid him five hundred and a bonus of two hundred three years later. If that's not enough! What does he want for goodness' sake?

TENCH. [*Complainingly*] Company made a hundred thousand out of his brains, and paid him seven hundred—that's the way he goes on, sir.

WILDER. The man's a rank agitator! Look here, I hate the Unions. But now we've got Harness here let's get him to settle the whole thing.

ANTHONY. No! [*Again they look at him.*

UNDERWOOD. Roberts won't let the men assent to that.

SCANTLEBURY. Fanatic! Fanatic!

WILDER. [*Looking at* ANTHONY] And not the only one!

[FROST *enters from the hall.*

FROST. [*To* ANTHONY] Mr. Harness from the Union, waiting, sir. The men are here too, sir.

[ANTHONY *nods.* UNDERWOOD *goes to the door, returning with* HARNESS, *a pale, clean-shaven man with hollow cheeks, quick eyes and lantern jaw*—FROST *has retired.*

UNDERWOOD. [*Pointing to* TENCH'S *chair*] Sit there next the Chairman, Harness, won't you?

[*At* HARNESS'S *appearance, the Board have drawn together, as it were, and turned a little to him, like cattle at a dog.*

HARNESS. [*With a sharp look round, and a bow*] Thanks! [*He sits—his accent is slightly nasal.*] Well, gentlemen, we're going to do business at last, I hope.

WILDER. Depends on what you *call* business, Harness. Why don't you make the men come in?

HARNESS. [*Sardonically*] The men are far more in the right than you are. The question with us is whether we shan't begin to support them again.

[*He ignores them all, except* ANTHONY, *to whom he turns in speaking.*

ANTHONY. Support them if you like; we'll put in free labour and have done with it.

HARNESS. That won't do, Mr. Anthony. You can't get free labour, and you know it.

ANTHONY. We shall see that.

HARNESS. I'm quite frank with you. We were forced to withhold our support from your men because some of their demands are in excess of current rates. I expect to make them withdraw those demands to-day: if they do, take it straight from me, gentlemen, we shall back them again at once. Now, I want to see something fixed up before I go back to-night. Can't we have done with this old-fashioned tug-of-war business? What good's it doing you? Why don't you recognize once for all that these people are men like yourselves, and want what's good for them just as you want what's good for you—— [*Bitterly*.]   Your motor-cars, and champagne, and eight-course dinners.

ANTHONY.   If the men will come in, we'll do something for them.

HARNESS.   [*Ironically*] Is that your opinion too, sir—and yours—and yours?   [*The Directors do not answer*.]   Well, all I can say is: It's a kind of high and mighty aristocratic tone I thought we'd grown out of—seems I was mistaken.

ANTHONY.   It's the tone the men use.   Remains to be seen which can hold out longest—they without us, or we without them.

HARNESS.   As business men, I wonder you're not ashamed of this waste of force, gentlemen.   You know what it'll all end in.

ANTHONY.   What?

HARNESS.   Compromise—it always does.

SCANTLEBURY.   Can't you persuade the men that their interests are the same as ours?

HARNESS.   [*Turning ironically*] I could persuade them of that, sir, if they were.

WILDER.   Come, Harness, you're a clever man, you don't believe all the Socialistic claptrap that's talked nowadays. There's no real difference between their interests and ours.

HARNESS.   There's just one very simple little question I'd like to put to you.   Will you pay your men one penny more than they force you to pay them?   [WILDER *is silent*.

WANKLIN.   [*Chiming in*] I humbly thought that not to pay more than was necessary was the A B C of commerce.

HARNESS.   [*With irony*] Yes, that seems to be the A B C of commerce, sir; and the A B C of commerce is between your interests and the men's.

SCANTLEBURY.   [*Whispering*] We ought to arrange something.

HARNESS.   [*Dryly*] Am I to understand then, gentlemen, that your Board is going to make no concessions?

[WANKLIN *and* WILDER *bend forward as if to speak, but stop.*
ANTHONY. [*Nodding*] None.
[WANKLIN *and* WILDER *again bend forward, and* SCANTLE-
BURY *gives an unexpected grunt.*
HARNESS. You were about to say something, I believe?
[*But* SCANTLEBURY *says nothing.*
EDGAR. [*Looking up suddenly*] We're sorry for the state of
the men.
HARNESS. [*Icily*] The men have no use for your pity, sir.
What they want is justice.
ANTHONY. Then let *them* be just.
HARNESS. For that word "just" read "humble," Mr.
Anthony. Why should they be humble? Barring the accident
of money, aren't they as good men as you?
ANTHONY. Cant!
HARNESS. Well, I've been five years in America. It
colours a man's notions.
SCANTLEBURY. [*Suddenly, as though avenging his uncompleted
grunt*] Let's have the men in and hear what they've got to say!
[ANTHONY *nods, and* UNDERWOOD *goes out by the single door.*
HARNESS. [*Dryly*] As I'm to have an interview with them
this afternoon, gentlemen, I'll ask you to postpone your final
decision till that's over.
[*Again* ANTHONY *nods, and taking up his glass drinks.*
[UNDERWOOD *comes in again, followed by* ROBERTS, GREEN,
BULGIN, THOMAS, ROUS. *They file in, hat in hand, and stand
silent in a row.* ROBERTS *is lean, of middle height, with a slight
stoop. He has a little rat-gnawn, brown-grey beard, moustaches,
high cheek-bones, hollow cheeks, small fiery eyes. He wears an old
and grease-stained blue serge suit, and carries an old bowler hat.
He stands nearest the Chairman.* GREEN, *next to him, has a
clean, worn face, with a small grey goatee beard and drooping
moustaches, iron spectacles, and mild, straightforward eyes. He
wears an overcoat, green with age, and a linen collar. Next to
him is* BULGIN, *a tall, strong man, with a dark moustache, and
fighting jaw, wearing a red muffler, who keeps changing his cap*

from one hand to the other.   Next to him is THOMAS, *an old man with a grey moustache, full beard, and weatherbeaten, bony face, whose overcoat discloses a lean, plucked-looking neck.   On his right,* ROUS, *the youngest of the five, looks like a soldier; he has a glitter in his eyes.*

UNDERWOOD.   [*Pointing*] There are some chairs there against the wall, Roberts; won't you draw them up and sit down?

ROBERTS.   Thank you, Mr. Underwood; we'll stand—in the presence of the Board.   [*He speaks in a biting and staccato voice, rolling his r's, pronouncing his a's like an Italian a, and his consonants short and crisp.*]   How are you, Mr. Harness? Didn't expect t' have the pleasure of seeing you till this afternoon.

HARNESS.   [*Steadily*] We shall meet again then, Roberts.

ROBERTS.   Glad to hear that; we shall have some news for you to take to your people.

ANTHONY.   What do the men want?

ROBERTS.   [*Acidly*] Beg pardon, I don't quite catch the Chairman's remark.

TENCH.   [*From behind the Chairman's chair*] The Chairman wishes to know what the men have to say.

ROBERTS.   It's what the Board has to say we've come to hear.   It's for the Board to speak first.

ANTHONY.   The Board has nothing to say.

ROBERTS.   [*Looking along the line of men*] In that case we're wasting the Directors' time.   We'll be taking our feet off this pretty carpet.

[*He turns, the men move slowly, as though hypnotically influenced.*

WANKLIN.   [*Suavely*] Come, Roberts, you didn't give us this long cold journey for the pleasure of saying that.

THOMAS.   [*A pure Welshman*] No, sir, an' what I say iss——

ROBERTS.   [*Bitingly*] Go on, Henry Thomas, go on. You're better able to speak to the—Directors than me.

[THOMAS *is silent.*

TENCH.   The Chairman means, Roberts, that it was the men who asked for the Conference, the Board wish to hear what they have to say.

ROBERTS.   Gad!   If I was to begin to tell ye all they have to say, I wouldn't be finished to-day.   And there'd be some that'd wish they'd never left their London palaces.

HARNESS.   What's your proposition, man?   Be reasonable.

ROBERTS.   You want reason, Mr. Harness?   Take a look round this afternoon before the meeting.   [*He looks at the men; no sound escapes them.*]   You'll see some very pretty scenery.

HARNESS.   All right, my friend; you won't put me off.

ROBERTS.   [*To the men*] We shan't put Mr. Harness off. Have some champagne with your lunch, Mr. Harness; you'll want it, sir.

HARNESS.   Come, get to business, man!

THOMAS.   What we're asking, look you, is just simple justice.

ROBERTS.   [*Venomously*] Justice from London?   What are you talking about, Henry Thomas?   Have you gone silly? [THOMAS *is silent.*]   We know very well what we are—discontented dogs—never satisfied.   What did the Chairman tell me up in London?   That I didn't know what I was talking about.   I was a foolish, uneducated man, that knew nothing of the wants of the men I spoke for.

EDGAR.   Do please keep to the point.

ANTHONY.   [*Holding up his hand*] There can only be one master, Roberts.

ROBERTS.   Then, be Gad, it'll be us.

[*There is a silence;* ANTHONY *and* ROBERTS *stare at one another.*

UNDERWOOD.   If you've nothing to say to the Directors, Roberts, perhaps you'll let Green or Thomas speak for the men.

[GREEN *and* THOMAS *look anxiously at* ROBERTS, *at each other, and the other men.*

GREEN.   [*An Englishman*] If I'd been listened to, gentlemen——

THOMAS.   What I'fe got to say iss what we'fe all got to say——

ROBERTS.   Speak for yourself, Henry Thomas.

SCANTLEBURY.   [*With a gesture of deep spiritual discomfort*] Let the poor men call their souls their own!

ROBERTS. Aye, they shall keep their souls, for it's not much body that you've left them, Mr. [*with biting emphasis, as though the word were an offence*] Scantlebury! [*To the men*] Well, will you speak, or shall I speak for you?

ROUS. [*Suddenly*] Speak out, Roberts, or leave it to others.

ROBERTS. [*Ironically*] Thank you, George Rous. [*Adressing himself to* ANTHONY.] The Chairman and Board of Directors have honoured us by leaving London and coming all this way to hear what we've got to say; it would not be polite to keep them any longer waiting.

WILDER. Well, thank God for that!

ROBERTS. Ye will not dare to thank Him when I have done, Mr. Wilder, for all your piety. May be your God up in London has no time to listen to the working man. I'm told He is a wealthy God; but if He listens to what I tell Him, He will know more than ever He learned in Kensington.

HARNESS. Come, Roberts, you have your own God. Respect the God of other men.

ROBERTS. That's right, sir. We have another God down here; I doubt He is rather different to Mr. Wilder's. Ask Henry Thomas; he will tell you whether his God and Mr. Wilder's are the same.

[THOMAS *lifts his hand, and cranes his head as though to prophesy.*

WANKLIN. For goodness' sake, let's keep to the point, Roberts.

ROBERTS. I rather think it is the point, Mr. Wanklin. If you can get the God of Capital to walk through the streets of Labour, and pay attention to what he sees, you're a brighter man than I take you for, for all that you're a Radical.

ANTHONY. Attend to me, Roberts! [ROBERTS *is silent.*] You are here to speak for the men, as I am here to speak for the Board. [*He looks slowly round.*] [WILDER, WANKLIN, *and* SCANTLEBURY *make movements of uneasiness, and* EDGAR *gazes at the floor. A faint smile comes on* HARNESS' *face.*] Now then, what is it?

ROBERTS. Right, sir? [*Throughout all that follows, he and* ANTHONY *look fixedly upon each other. Men and Directors show in their various ways suppressed uneasiness, as though listening to words that they themselves would not have spoken.*] The men can't afford to travel up to London; and they don't trust you to believe what they say in black and white. They know what the post is [*he darts a look at* UNDERWOOD *and* TENCH], and what Directors' meetings are: "Refer it to the manager—let the manager advise us on the men's condition. Can we squeeze them a little more?"

UNDERWOOD. [*In a low voice*] Don't hit below the belt, Roberts!

ROBERTS. Is it below the belt, Mr. Underwood? The men know. When I came up to London, I told you the position straight. An' what came of it? I was told I didn't know what I was talkin' about. I can't afford to travel up to London to be told that again.

ANTHONY. What have you to say for the men?

ROBERTS. I have this to say—and first as to their condition. Ye shall 'ave no need to go and ask your manager. Ye can't squeeze them any more. Every man of us is well-nigh starving. [*A surprised murmur rises from the men.* ROBERTS *looks round.*] Ye wonder why I tell ye that? Every man of us is going short. We can't be no worse off than we've been these weeks past. Ye needn't think that by waiting ye'll drive us to come in. We'll die first, the whole lot of us. The men have sent for ye to know, once and for all, whether ye are going to grant them their demands. I see the sheet of paper in the Secretary's hand. [TENCH *moves nervously.*] That's it, I think, Mr. Tench. It's not very large.

TENCH. [*Nodding*] Yes.

ROBERTS. There's not one sentence of writing on that paper that we can do without. [*A movement amongst the men.* ROBERTS *turns on them sharply*] Isn't that so?" [*The men assent reluctantly.* ANTHONY *takes from* TENCH *the paper and peruses it.*] Not one single sentence. All those demands are fair. We have not asked anything that we are not entitled to ask. What I said up in London, I say again now: there is not anything on that piece of paper that a just man should not ask, and a just man give. [*A pause.*

ANTHONY. There is not one single demand on this paper that we will grant.

[*In the stir that follows on these words,* ROBERTS *watches the Directors and* ANTHONY *the men.* WILDER *gets up abruptly and goes over to the fire.*

ROBERTS. D'ye mean that?

ANTHONY. I do.

[WILDER *at the fire makes an emphatic movement of disgust.*

ROBERTS. [*Noting it, with dry intensity*] Ye best know whether the condition of the Company is any better than the condition of the men. [*Scanning the Directors' faces.*] Ye best know whether ye can afford your tyranny—but this I tell ye: If ye think the men will give way the least part of an inch, ye're making the worst mistake ye ever made. [*He fixes his eyes on* SCANTLEBURY.] Ye think because the Union is not supporting us —more shame to it!—that we'll be coming on our knees to you one fine morning. Ye think because the men have got their wives an' families to think of—that it's just a question of a week or two——

ANTHONY. It would be better if you did not speculate so much on what we think.

ROBERTS. Aye! It's not much profit to us! I will say this for you, Mr. Anthony—ye know your own mind! [*Staring at* ANTHONY.] I can reckon on ye!

ANTHONY. [*Ironically*] I am obliged to you!

ROBERTS. And I know mine. I tell ye this. The men will send their wives and families where the country will have to keep them; an' they will starve sooner than give way. I advise ye, Mr. Anthony, to prepare yourself for the worst that can happen to your Company. We are not so ignorant as you might suppose. We know the way the cat is jumping. Your position is not all that it might be—not exactly!

ANTHONY. Be good enough to allow us to judge of our position for ourselves.   Go back, and reconsider your own.

ROBERTS. [*Stepping forward*] Mr. Anthony, you are not a young man now; from the time that I remember anything ye have been an enemy to every man that has come into your works. I don't say that ye're a mean man, or a cruel man, but ye've grudged them the say of any word in their own fate.   Ye've fought them down four times.   I've heard ye say ye love a fight—mark my words—ye're fighting the last fight ye'll ever fight——   [TENCH *touches* ROBERTS' *sleeve.*

UNDERWOOD. Roberts! Roberts!

ROBERTS. Roberts! Roberts! I mustn't speak my mind to the Chairman, but the Chairman may speak his mind to me!

WILDER. What are things coming to?

ANTHONY. [*With a grim smile at* WILDER] Go on, Roberts; say what you like.

ROBERTS. [*After a pause*] I have no more to say.

ANTHONY. The meeting stands adjourned to five o'clock.

WANKLIN. [*In a low voice to* UNDERWOOD] We shall never settle anything like this.

ROBERTS. [*Bitingly*] We thank the Chairman and Board of Directors for their gracious hearing.

[*He moves towards the door; the men cluster together stupefied; then* ROUS, *throwing up his head, passes* ROBERTS *and goes out. The others follow.*

ROBERTS. [*With his hand on the door—maliciously*] Good day, gentlemen!   [*He goes out.*

HARNESS. [*Ironically*] I congratulate you on the conciliatory spirit that's been displayed.   With your permission, gentlemen, I'll be with you again at half-past five.   Good morning!

[*He bows slightly, rests his eyes on* ANTHONY, *who returns his stare unmoved, and, followed by* UNDERWOOD, *goes out.   There is a moment of uneasy silence.* UNDERWOOD *reappears in the doorway.*

WILDER. [*With emphatic disgust*] Well!

[*The double doors are opened.*

ENID. [*Standing in the doorway*] Lunch is ready.

[EDGAR, *getting up abruptly, walks out past his sister.*

WILDER. Coming to lunch, Scantlebury?

SCANTLEBURY. [*Rising heavily*] I suppose so, I suppose so. It's the only thing we can do.

[*They go out through the double doors.*

WANKLIN. [*In a low voice*] Do you really mean to fight to a finish, Chairman? [ANTHONY *nods.*

WANKLIN. Take care! The essence of things is to know when to stop. [ANTHONY *does not answer.*

WANKLIN. [*Very gravely*] This way disaster lies. The ancient Trojans were fools to your father, Mrs. Underwood.

[*He goes out through the double doors.*

ENID. I want to speak to father, Frank.

[UNDERWOOD *follows* WANKLIN *out.* TENCH, *passing round the table, is restoring order to the scattered pens and papers.*

ENID. Aren't you coming, Dad?

[ANTHONY *shakes his head.* ENID *looks meaningly at* TENCH.

ENID. Won't you go and have some lunch, Mr, Tench

TENCH. [*With papers in his hand*] Thank you, ma'am, thank you! [*He goes slowly, looking back.*

ENID. [*Shutting the doors*] I *do* hope it's settled, father!

ANTHONY. No!

ENID. [*Very disappointed*] Oh! Haven't you done anything? [ANTHONY *shakes his head.*

ENID. Frank says they all want to come to a compromise, really, except that man Roberts.

ANTHONY. *I* don't.

ENID. It's such a horrid position for us. If you were the wife of the manager, and lived down here, and saw it all. You can't realize, Dad!

ANTHONY. Indeed?

ENID. We see *all* the distress. You remember my maid Annie, who married Roberts? [ANTHONY *nods.*] It's so wretched, her heart's weak; since the strike began, she hasn't even been getting proper food. I know it for a fact, father.

ANTHONY. Give her what she wants, poor woman!

ENID. Roberts won't let her take anything from *us*.

ANTHONY. [*Staring before him*] I can't be answerable for the men's obstinacy.

ENID. They're all suffering. Father! Do stop it, for my sake!

ANTHONY. [*With a keen look at her*] You don't understand, my dear.

ENID. If I were on the Board, I'd do something.

ANTHONY. What would you do?

ENID. It's because you can't bear to give way. It's so——

ANTHONY. Well?

ENID. So unnecessary.

ANTHONY. What do *you* know about necessity? Read your novels, play your music, talk your talk, but don't try and tell *me* what's at the bottom of a struggle like this.

ENID. I live down here, and see it.

ANTHONY. What d'you imagine stands between you and your class and these men that you're so sorry for?

ENID. [*Coldly*] I don't know what you mean, father.

ANTHONY. In a few years you and your children would be down in the condition they're in, but for those who have the eyes to see things as they are and the backbone to stand up for themselves.

ENID. You don't know the state the men are in.

ANTHONY. I know it well enough.

ENID. You don't, father; if you did, you wouldn't——

ANTHONY. It's you who don't know the simple facts of the position. What sort of mercy do you suppose you'd get if no one stood between you and the continual demands of labour? This sort of mercy—[*he puts his hand up to his throat and squeezes it*]. First would go your sentiments, my dear; then your culture, and your comforts would be going all the time!

ENID. I don't believe in barriers between classes.

ANTHONY. You—don't—believe—in—barriers—between the classes?

ENID. [*Coldly*] And I don't know what that has to do with this question.

ANTHONY. It will take a generation or two for you to understand.

ENID. It's only you and Roberts, father, and you know it! [ANTHONY *thrusts out his lower lip.*] It'll ruin the Company.

ANTHONY. Allow me to judge of that.

ENID. [*Resentfully*] I won't stand by and let poor Annie Roberts suffer like this! And think of the children, father! I warn you.

ANTHONY. [*With a grim smile*] What do you propose to do?

ENID. That's my affair.. [ANTHONY *only looks at her.*

ENID. [*In a changed voice, stroking his sleeve*] Father, you *know* you oughtn't to have this strain on you—you know what Dr. Fisher said!

ANTHONY. No old man can afford to listen to old women.

ENID. But you *have* done enough, even if it really is such a matter of principle with you.

ANTHONY. You think so?

ENID. Don't, Dad! [*Her face works.*] You—you might think of *us*!

ANTHONY. I am.

ENID. It'll break you down.

ANTHONY. [*Slowly*] My dear, I am not going to funk; you may rely on that.

[*Re-enter* TENCH *with papers; he glances at them, then plucking up courage.*

TENCH. Beg pardon, Madam, I think I'd rather see these papers were disposed of before I get my lunch.

[ENID, *after an impatient glance at him, looks at her father, turns suddenly, and goes into the drawing-room.*

TENCH. [*Holding the papers and a pen to* ANTHONY, *very nervously*] Would you sign these for me, please sir?

[ANTHONY *takes the pen and signs.*

TENCH. [*Standing with a sheet of blotting-paper behind* EDGAR'S *chair, begins speaking nervously*] I owe my position to you, sir.

ANTHONY.   Well?

TENCH.   I'm obliged to see everything that's going on, sir;
I—I depend upon the Company entirely.   If anything were to
happen to it, it'd be disastrous for me. [ANTHONY *nods*.]   And,
of course, my wife's just had another; and so it makes me doubly
anxious just now.   And the rates are really terrible down our
way.

ANTHONY.   [*With grim amusement*] Not more terrible than
they are up mine.

TENCH.   No, sir? [*Very nervously*.]   I know the Company
means a great deal to you, sir.

ANTHONY.   It does; I founded it.

TENCH.   Yes, sir.   If the strike goes on it'll be very serious.
I think the Directors are beginning to realize that, sir.

ANTHONY.   [*Ironically*] Indeed?

TENCH.   I know you hold very strong views, sir, and it's
always your habit to look things in the face; but I don't think
the Directors—like it, sir, now they—they see it.

ANTHONY.   [*Grimly*] Nor you, it seems.

TENCH.   [*With the ghost of a smile*] No, sir; of course I've
got my children, and my wife's delicate; in my position I *have*
to think of these things.   [ANTHONY *nods*.]   It wasn't *that* I
was going to say, sir, if you'll excuse me [*hesitates*]——

ANTHONY.   Out with it, then!

TENCH.   I know—from my own father, sir, that when you
get on in life you do feel things dreadfully——

ANTHONY.   [*Almost paternally*] Come, out with it, Tench!

TENCH.   I don't *like* to say it, sir.

ANTHONY.   [*Stonily*] You must.

TENCH.   [*After a pause, desperately bolting it out*] I think
the Directors are going to throw you over, sir.

ANTHONY.   [*Sits in silence*] Ring the bell!

[TENCH *nervously rings the bell and stands by the fire.*

TENCH.   Excuse me saying such a thing.   I was *only*
thinking of you, sir.

[FROST *enters from the hall, he comes to the foot of the table, and looks at* ANTHONY; TENCH *covers his nervousness by arranging papers.*

ANTHONY.   Bring me a whisky and soda.

FROST.   Anything to eat, sir?

[ANTHONY *shakes his head*—FROST *goes to the sideboard, and prepares the drink.*

TENCH.   [*In a low voice, almost supplicating*] If you could see your way, sir, it would be a great relief to my mind, it would indeed. [*He looks up at* ANTHONY, *who has not moved.*] It does make me so very anxious. I haven't slept properly for weeks, sir, and that's a fact.

[ANTHONY *looks in his face, then slowly shakes his head.*

TENCH.   [*Disheartened*] No, sir? [*He goes on arranging papers.* FROST *places the whisky and soda on a salver and puts it down by* ANTHONY'S *right hand. He stands away, looking gravely at* ANTHONY.

FROST.   *Nothing* I can get you, sir? [ANTHONY *shakes his head.*] You're aware, sir, of what the doctor said, sir?

ANTHONY.   I am.

[*A pause.* FROST *suddenly moves closer to him, and speaks in a low voice.*

FROST.   This strike, sir; puttin' all this strain on you. Excuse me, sir, is it—is it worth it, sir? [ANTHONY *mutters some words that are inaudible.*] Very good, sir!

[*He turns and goes out into the hall*—TENCH *makes two attempts to speak; but meeting his Chairman's gaze he drops his eyes, and turning dismally, he too goes out.* ANTHONY *is left alone. He grips the glass, tilts it, and drinks deeply; then sets it down with a deep and rumbling sigh, and leans back in his chair.*

The curtain falls.

ACT II

SCENE I

It is half-past three. In the kitchen of ROBERTS' *cottage a meagre little fire is burning. The room is clean and tidy, very barely furnished, with a brick floor and white-washed walls, much stained with smoke. There is a kettle on the fire. A door opposite the fireplace opens inwards from a snowy street. On the wooden table are a cup and saucer, a teapot, knife, and plate of bread and cheese. Close to the fireplace in an old armchair, wrapped in a rug, sits* MRS. ROBERTS, *a thin and dark-haired woman about thirty-five, with patient eyes. Her hair is not done up, but tied back with a piece of ribbon. By the fire, too, is* MRS. YEO; *a red-haired, broad-faced person. Sitting near the table is* MRS. ROUS, *an old lady, ashen-white, with silver hair; by the door, standing, as if about to go, is* MRS. BULGIN, *a little pale, pinched-up woman. In a chair, with her elbows resting on the table and her face resting in her hands, sits* MADGE THOMAS, *a good-looking girl, of twenty-two, with high cheek-bones, deep-set eyes, and dark, untidy hair. She is listening to the talk but she neither speaks nor moves.*

MRS. YEO. So he give me a sixpence, and that's the first bit o' money *I* seen this week. There an't much 'eat to this fire. Come and warm yerself, Mrs. Rous, you're lookin' as white as the snow, you are.

MRS. ROUS. [*Shivering—placidly*] Ah! but the winter my old man was took was the proper winter. Seventy-nine that was, when none of you was hardly born—not Madge Thomas, nor Sue Bulgin. [*Looking at them in turn.*] Annie Roberts, 'ow old were you, dear?

MRS. ROBERTS. Seven, Mrs. Rous.

26

Mrs. Rous. Seven—well ther'! A tiny little thing!

Mrs. Yeo. [*Aggressively*] Well, I was ten myself, *I* remembers it.

Mrs. Rous. [*Placidly*] The Company hadn't been started three years. Father was workin' on the acid that's 'ow he got 'is pisoned leg. I kep' sayin' to 'im "Father, you've got a pisoned leg." "Well," 'e said, "Mother, pison or no pison, I can't afford to go a-layin' up." An' two days after he was on 'is back, and never got up again. It was Providence! There wasn't none o' these Compensation Acts then.

Mrs. Yeo. Ye hadn't no strike that winter! [*With grim humour.*] This winter's 'ard enough for me. Mrs. Roberts, you don't want no 'arder winter, do you? Wouldn't seem natural to 'ave a dinner, would it, Mrs. Bulgin?

Mrs. Bulgin. We've had bread and tea last four days.

Mrs. Yeo. You got that Friday's laundry job?

Mrs. Bulgin. [*Dispiritedly*] They said they'd give it me, but when I went last Friday, they were full up. I got to go again next week.

Mrs. Yeo. Ah! There's too many after that. I send Yeo out on the ice to put on the gentry's skates an' pick up what 'e can. Stops 'im from broodin' about the 'ouse.

Mrs. Bulgin. [*In a desolate, matter-of-fact voice*] Leavin' out the men—it's bad enough with the children. I keep 'em in bed, they don't get so hungry when they're not running about; but they're that restless in bed they worry your life out.

Mrs. Yeo. You're lucky they're all so small. It's the goin' to school that makes 'em 'ungry. Don't Bulgin give you *anythin'*?

Mrs. Bulgin. [*Shakes her head, then, as though by after-thought*] Would if he could, I s'pose.

Mrs. Yeo. [*Sardonically*] What! 'Aven't 'e got no shares in the Company?

Mrs. Rous. [*Rising with tremendous cheerfulness*] Well, good-bye, Annie Roberts, I'm going along home.

Mrs. Roberts. Stay an' have a cup of tea, Mrs. Rous?

Mrs. Rous. [*With the faintest smile*] Roberts'll want 'is tea when he comes in. I'll just go an' get to bed; it's warmer there than anywhere.   [*She moves very shakily towards the door.*

Mrs. Yeo. [*Rising and giving her an arm*] Come on, Mother, take my arm; we're all goin' the same way.

Mrs. Rous. [*Taking the arm*] Thank you, my dearies!

[*They go out, followed by* Mrs. Bulgin.

Madge. [*Moving for the first time*] There, Annie, you see that! I told George Rous, "Don't think to have my company till you've made an end of all this trouble. You ought to be ashamed," I said, "with your own mother looking like a ghost, and not a stick to put on the fire. So long as you're able to fill your pipes, you'll let us starve." "I'll take my oath, Madge," he said, "I've not had smoke nor drink these three weeks!" "Well, then, why do you go on with it?" "I can't go back on Roberts!" . . . That's it! Roberts, always Roberts! They'd all drop it but for him. When *he* talks it's the devil that comes into them. [*A silence.* Mrs. Roberts *makes a movement of pain.*] Ah! *You* don't want him beaten! He's your man. With everybody like their own shadows! [*She makes a gesture towards* Mrs. Roberts.] If Rous wants me he must give up Roberts. If *he* gave him up—they all would. They're only waiting for a lead. Father's against him—they're all against him in their hearts.

Mrs. Roberts. You won't beat Roberts! [*They look silently at each other.*]

Madge. Won't I? The cowards—when their own mothers and their own children don't know where to turn.

Mrs. Roberts. Madge!

Madge. [*Looking searchingly at* Mrs. Roberts] I wonder he can look *you* in the face. [*She squats before the fire, with her hands out to the flame.*] Harness is here again. They'll have to make up their minds to-day.

Mrs. Roberts. [*In a soft, slow voice, with a slight West-country burr*] Roberts will never give up the furnacemen and engineers. 'Twouldn't be right.

MADGE. You can't deceive me. It's just his pride.

[*A tapping at the door is heard, the women turn as* ENID *enters. She wears a round fur cap, and a jacket of squirrel's fur. She closes the door behind her.*

ENID. Can I come in, Annie?

MRS. ROBERTS. [*Flinching*] Miss Enid! Give Mrs. Underwood a chair, Madge.

[MADGE *gives* ENID *the chair she has been sitting on.*

ENID. Thank you!

ENID. Are you any better?

MRS. ROBERTS. Yes, M'm; thank you, M'm.

ENID. [*Looking at the sullen* MADGE *as though requesting her departure*] Why did you send back the jelly? I call that really wicked of you!

MRS. ROBERTS. Thank you, M'm, I'd no need for it.

ENID. Of course! It was Roberts' doing, wasn't it? How can he let all this suffering go on amongst you?

MADGE. [*Suddenly*] What suffering?

ENID. [*Surprised*] I beg your pardon!

MADGE. Who said there was suffering?

MRS. ROBERTS. Madge?

MADGE. [*Throwing her shawl over her head*] Please to let us keep ourselves to ourselves. We don't want you coming here and spying on us.

ENID. [*Confronting her, but without rising*] I didn't speak to you.

MADGE. [*In a low, fierce voice*] Keep your kind feelings to yourself. You think you can come amongst us, but you're mistaken. Go back and tell the Manager that.

ENID. [*Stonily*] This is not your house.

MADGE. [*Turning to the door*] No, it is not my house; keep clear of my house, Mrs. Underwood.

[*She goes out.* ENID *taps her fingers on the table.*

MRS. ROBERTS. Please to forgive Madge Thomas, M'm; she's a bit upset to-day. [*A pause.*

ENID. [*Looking at her*] Oh, I think they're so *stupid*, all of them.

MRS. ROBERTS.   [*With a faint smile*] Yes, M'm.

ENID.   Is Roberts out?

MRS. ROBERTS.   Yes, M'm.

ENID.   It is *his doing*, that they don't come to an agreement. Now isn't it, Annie?

MRS. ROBERTS.   [*Softly, with her eyes on* ENID, *and moving the fingers of one hand continually on her breast*] They do say that your father, M'm——

ENID.   My father's getting an old man, and you know what old men are.

MRS. ROBERTS.   I am sorry, M'm.

ENID.   [*More softly*] I don't expect *you* to feel sorry, Annie. I know it's his fault as well as Roberts'.

MRS. ROBERTS.   I'm sorry for anyone that gets old, M'm; it's dreadful to get old, and Mr. Anthony was such a fine old man I always used to think.

ENID.   [*Impulsively*] He always liked you, don't you remember?   Look here, Annie, what can I do?   I do so want to know.   You don't get what you ought to have.   [*Going to the fire, she takes the kettle off, and looks for coals.*]   And you're so naughty sending back the soup and things!

MRS. ROBERTS.   [*With a faint smile*] Yes, M'm?

ENID.   [*Resentfully*] Why, you haven't even got coals?

MRS. ROBERTS.   If you please, M'm, to put the kettle on again; Roberts won't have long for his tea when he comes in. He's got to meet the men at four.

ENID.   [*Putting the kettle on*] That means he'll lash them into a fury again.   Can't you stop his going, Annie? [MRS. ROBERTS *smiles ironically.*]   Have you tried?   [*A silence.*]   Does he know how ill you are?

MRS. ROBERTS.   It's only my weak 'eart, M'm.

ENID.   You used to be so well when you were with us.

MRS. ROBERTS.   [*Stiffening*] Roberts is always good to me.

ENID.   But you ought to have everything you want, and you have nothing!

Mrs. Roberts. [*Appealingly*] They tell me I don't look like a dyin' woman?

Enid. Of course you don't; if you could only have proper—— Will you see my doctor if I send him to you? I'm sure he'd do you good.

Mrs. Roberts. [*With faint questioning*] Yes, M'm.

Enid. Madge Thomas oughtn't to come here; she only excites you. As if I didn't know what suffering there is amongst the men! I do feel for them dreadfully, but you know they *have* gone too far.

Mrs. Roberts. [*Continually moving her fingers*] They say there's no other way to get better wages, M'm.

Enid. [*Earnestly*] But, Annie, that's why the Union won't help them. My husband's very sympathetic with the men, but he says they're not underpaid.

Mrs. Roberts. No, M'm?

Enid. They never think how the Company could go on if we paid the wages they want.

Mrs. Roberts. [*With an effort*] But the dividends having been so big, M'm.

Enid. [*Taken aback*] You all seem to think the shareholders are rich men, but they're not—most of them are really no better off than working men. [Mrs. Roberts *smiles.*] They have to keep up appearances.

Mrs. Roberts. Yes, M'm?

Enid. You don't have to pay rates and taxes, and a hundred other things that they do. If the men didn't spend such a lot in drink and betting they'd be quite well off!

Mrs. Roberts. They say, workin' so hard, they must have some pleasure.

Enid. But surely not low pleasure like that.

Mrs. Roberts. [*A little resentfully*] Roberts never touches a drop; and he's never had a bet in his life.

Enid. Oh! but he's not a com—— I mean he's an engineer —a superior man.

MRS. ROBERTS. Yes, M'm. Roberts says they've no chance of other pleasures.

ENID. [*Musing*] Of course, I know it's hard.

MRS. ROBERTS. [*With a spice of malice*] And they say gentlefolk's just as bad.

ENID. [*With a smile*] I go as far as most people, Annie, but you know, yourself, that's nonsense.

MRS. ROBERTS. [*With painful effort*] A lot o' the men never go near the Public; but even they don't save but very little, and that goes if there's illness.

ENID. But they've got their clubs, haven't they?

MRS. ROBERTS. The clubs only give up to eighteen shillin's a week, M'm, and it's not much amongst a family. Roberts says workin' folk have always lived from hand to mouth. Sixpence to-day is worth more than a shillin' to-morrow, that's what they say.

ENID. But that's the spirit of gambling.

MRS. ROBERTS. [*With a sort of excitement*] Roberts says a working man's life is all a gamble, from the time 'e's born to the time 'e dies. [ENID *leans forward, interested.* MRS. ROBERTS *goes on with a growing excitement that culminates in the personal feeling of the last words.*] He says, M'm, that when a working man's baby is born, it's a toss-up from breath to breath whether it ever draws another, and so on all 'is life; an' when he comes to be old, it's the workhouse or the grave. He says that without a man is very near, and pinches and stints 'imself and 'is children to save, there can't be neither surplus nor security. That's why he wouldn't have no children [*she sinks back*], not though I *wanted* them.

ENID. Yes, yes, I know!

MRS. ROBERTS. No, you don't, M'm. You've got your children, and you'll never need to trouble for them.

ENID. [*Gently*] You oughtn't to be talking so much, Annie. [*Then, in spite of herself.*] But Roberts was paid a lot of money, wasn't he, for discovering that process?

MRS. ROBERTS. [*On the defensive*] All Roberts' savin's have gone. He's always looked forward to this strike. He says he's no right to a farthing when the others are suffering. 'Tisn't so with all o' them! Some don't seem to care no more than that— so long as they get their own.

ENID. I don't see how they can be expected to when they're suffering like this. [*In a changed voice.*] But Roberts ought to think of *you*! It's all terrible! The kettle's boiling. Shall I make the tea? [*She takes the teapot, and seeing tea there, pours water into it.*] Won't you have a cup?

MRS. ROBERTS. No, thank you, M'm. [*She is listening, as though for footsteps.*] I'd sooner you didn't see Roberts, M'm, he gets so wild.

ENID. Oh! but I must, Annie; I'll be quite calm, I promise.

MRS. ROBERTS. It's life an' death to him, M'm.

ENID. [*Very gently*] I'll get him to talk to me outside, we won't excite you.

MRS. ROBERTS. [*Faintly*] No, M'm.

[*She gives a violent start.* ROBERTS *has come in, unseen.*

ROBERTS. [*Removing his hat—with subtle mockery*] Beg pardon for coming in; you're engaged with a lady, I see.

ENID. Can I speak to you, Mr. Roberts?

ROBERTS. Whom have I the pleasure of addressing, Ma'am?

ENID. But surely you know me! I'm Mrs. Underwood.

ROBERTS. [*With a bow of malice*] The daughter of our chairman.

ENID. [*Earnestly*] I've come on purpose to speak to you; will you come outside a minute? [*She looks at* MRS. ROBERTS.

ROBERTS. [*Hanging up his hat*] I have nothing to say, Ma'am.

ENID. But I *must* speak to you, please.

[*She moves towards the door.*

ROBERTS. [*With sudden venom*] I have not the time to listen!

MRS. ROBERTS. David!

ENID. Mr. Roberts, *please*!

ROBERTS. [*Taking off his overcoat*] I am sorry to disoblige a lady—Mr. Anthony's daughter.

ENID. [*Wavering, then with sudden decision*] Mr. Roberts,

I know you've another meeting of the men. [ROBERTS *bows.*]
I came to appeal to you. Please, please try to come to some
compromise; give way a little, if it's only for your own sakes!

ROBERTS. [*Speaking to himself*] The daughter of Mr. Anthony
begs me to give way a little, if it's only for our own sakes.

ENID. For everybody's sake; for your wife's sake.

ROBERTS. For my wife's sake, for everybody's sake—for
the sake of Mr. Anthony.

ENID. Why are you so bitter against my father? He has
never done anything to you.

ROBERTS. Has he not?

ENID. He can't help his views, any more than you can help
yours.

ROBERTS. I really didn't know that I had a right to views!

ENID. He's an old man, and you——

                                   [*Seeing his eyes fixed on her, she stops.*

ROBERTS. [*Without raising his voice*] If I saw Mr. Anthony
going to die, and I could save him by lifting my hand, I would
not lift the little finger of it.

ENID. You—you——   [*She stops again, biting her lips.*

ROBERTS. I would not, and that's flat!

ENID. [*Coldly*] You don't mean what you say, and you
know it!

ROBERTS. I mean every word of it.

ENID. But why?

ROBERTS. [*With a flash*] Mr. Anthony stands for tyranny!
That's why!

ENID. Nonsense!

[MRS. ROBERTS *makes a movement as if to rise, but sinks back
in her chair.*

ENID. [*With an impetuous movement*] Annie!

ROBERTS. Please not to touch my wife!

ENID. [*Recoiling with a sort of horror*] I believe—you are mad.

ROBERTS. The house of a madman then is not the fit place
for a lady.

ENID. I'm not afraid of you.

ROBERTS. [*Bowing*] I would not expect the daughter of Mr. Anthony to be afraid. Mr. Anthony is not a coward like the rest of them.

ENID. [*Suddenly*] I suppose you think it brave, then, to go on with this struggle.

ROBERTS. Does Mr. Anthony think it brave to fight against women and children? Mr. Anthony is a rich man, I believe; does he think it brave to fight against those who haven't a penny? Does he think it brave to set children crying with hunger, an' women shivering with cold?

ENID. [*Putting up her hand, as though warding off a blow*] My father is acting on his principles, and you know it!

ROBERTS. And so am I!

ENID. You hate us; and you can't bear to be beaten.

ROBERTS. Neither can Mr. Anthony, for all that he may say.

ENID. At any rate you might have pity on your wife.

[MRS. ROBERTS, *who has her hand pressed to her heart, takes it away, and tries to calm her breathing.*

ROBERTS. Madam, I have no more to say.

[*He takes up the loaf. There is a knock at the door, and* UNDERWOOD *comes in. He stands looking at them,* ENID *turns to him, then seems undecided.*

UNDERWOOD. Enid!

ROBERTS. [*Ironically*] Ye were not needing to come for your wife, Mr. Underwood. We are not rowdies.

UNDERWOOD. I know that, Roberts. I hope Mrs. Roberts is better. [ROBERTS *turns away without answering.*] Come, Enid!

ENID. I make one more appeal to you, Mr. Roberts, for the sake of your wife.

ROBERTS. [*With polite malice*] If I might advise ye, Ma'am —make it for the sake of your husband and your father.

[ENID, *suppressing a retort, goes out.* UNDERWOOD *opens the door for her and follows.* ROBERTS, *going to the fire, holds out his hands to the dying glow.*

ROBERTS. How goes it, my girl? Feeling better, are you? [MRS. ROBERTS *smiles faintly. He brings his overcoat and*

wraps it round her.] [*Looking at his watch.*] Ten minutes to
four! [*As though inspired.*] I've seen their faces, there's no
fight in them, except for that one old robber.

MRS. ROBERTS. Won't you stop and eat, David? You've
'ad nothing all day!

ROBERTS. [*Putting his hand to his throat*] Can't swallow till
those old sharks are out o' the town. [*He walks up and down.*]
I shall have a bother with the men—there's no heart in them,
the cowards. Blind as bats, they are—can't see a day before
their noses.

MRS. ROBERTS. It's the women, David.

ROBERTS. Ah! So they say! They can remember the
women when their own bellies speak! The women never stop
them from the drink; but from a little suffering to themselves in
a sacred cause, the women stop them fast enough.

MRS. ROBERTS. But think o' the children, David.

ROBERTS. Ah! If they will go breeding themselves for
slaves, without a thought o' the future o' them they breed——

MRS. ROBERTS. [*Gasping*] That's enough, David; don't
begin to talk of that—I won't—I can't——

ROBERTS. [*Staring at her*] Now, now, my girl!

MRS. ROBERTS. [*Breathlessly*] No, no, David—I won't!

ROBERTS. There, there! Come, come! That's right.
[*Bitterly.*] Not one penny will they put by for a day like this.
Not they! Hand to mouth—Gad!—I know them! They've
broke my heart. There was no holdin' them at the start, but
now the pinch 'as come.

MRS. ROBERTS. How can you expect it, David? They're
not made of iron.

ROBERTS. Expect it? Wouldn't I expect what I would do
meself? Wouldn't I starve an' rot rather than give in? What
one man can do, another can.

MRS. ROBERTS. And the women?

ROBERTS. This is not women's work.

MRS. ROBERTS. [*With a flash of malice*] No, the women
may die for all you care. That's their work.

ROBERTS. [*Averting his eyes*] Who talks of dying? No one will die till we have beaten these—— [*He meets her eyes again, and again turns his away. Excitedly.*] This is what I've been waiting for all these months. To get the old robbers down, and send them home again without a farthin's worth o' change. I've seen their faces, I tell you, in the valley of the shadow of defeat. [*He goes to the peg and takes down his hat.*

MRS. ROBERTS. [*Following with her eyes—softly*] Take your overcoat, David; it must be bitter cold.

ROBERTS. [*Coming up to her—his eyes are furtive*] No, no! There, there, stay quiet and warm. I won't be long, my girl!

MRS. ROBERTS. [*With soft bitterness*] You'd better take it.

[*She lifts the coat. But* ROBERTS *puts it back, and wraps it round her. He tries to meet her eyes, but cannot.* MRS. ROBERTS *stays huddled in the coat, her eyes, that follow him about, are half malicious, half yearning. He looks at his watch again, and turns to go. In the doorway he meets* JAN THOMAS, *a boy of ten in clothes too big for him, carrying a penny whistle.*

ROBERTS. Hallo, boy!

[*He goes,* JAN *stops within a yard of* MRS. ROBERTS, *and stares at her without a word.*

MRS. ROBERTS. Well, Jan!

JAN. Father's coming; sister Madge is coming.

[*He sits at the table, and fidgets with his whistle; he blows three vague notes; then imitates a cuckoo.*

[*There is a tap on the door. Old* THOMAS *comes in.*

THOMAS. A very coot tay to you, Ma'am. It is petter that you are.

MRS. ROBERTS. Thank you, Mr. Thomas.

THOMAS. [*Nervously*] Roberts in?

MRS. ROBERTS. Just gone on to the meeting, Mr. Thomas.

THOMAS. [*With relief, becoming talkative*] This is fery unfortunate, look you! I came to tell him that we must make terms with London. It is a fery great pity he is gone to the meeting. He will be kicking against the pricks, I am thinking.

Mrs. Roberts. [*Half rising*] He'll never give in, Mr. Thomas.

Thomas. You must not be fretting, that is very pat for you. Look you, there iss hartly any mans for supporting him now, but the engineers and George Rous. [*Solemnly.*] This strike is no longer coing with Chapel, look you! I have listened carefully, an' I have talked with her. [Jan *blows.*] Sst! I don't care what th' others say, I say that *Chapel means us* to be stopping the trouble, that is what I make of her; and it is my opinion that this is the fery best thing for all of us. If it wasn't my opinion, I ton't say—but it is my opinion, look you.

Mrs. Roberts. [*Trying to suppress her excitement*] I don't know what'll come to Roberts, if you give in.

Thomas. It iss no disgrace whateffer! All that a mortal man coult do he hass tone. It iss against Human Nature he hass gone; fery natural—any man may to that; but Chapel has spoken and he must not co against *her.*   [Jan *imitates the cuckoo.*] Ton't make that squeaking! [*Going to the door.*] Here iss my taughter come to sit with you. A fery goot day, Ma'am—no fretting—rememper!

[Madge *comes in and stands at the open door, watching the street.*

Madge. You'll be late, Father; they're beginning. [*She catches him by the sleeve.*] For the love of God, stand up to him, Father—this time!

Thomas. [*Detaching his sleeve with dignity*] Leave me to do what's proper, girl!

[*He goes out,* Madge, *in the centre of the open doorway, slowly moves in, as though before the approach of someone.*

Rous. [*Appearing in the doorway*] Madge! [Madge *stands with her back to* Mrs. Roberts, *staring at him with her head up and her hands behind her.*

Rous. [*Who has a fierce distracted look*] Madge! I'm going to the meeting. [Madge, *without moving, smiles contemptuously.*] D'ye hear me?   [*They speak in quick low voices.*

Madge. I hear! Go, and kill your own Mother, if you must.

[ROUS *seizes her by both her arms. She stands rigid, with her head bent back. He releases her, and he too stands motionless.*

ROUS. I swore to stand by Roberts. I swore that! Ye want me to go back on what I've sworn.

MADGE. [*With slow soft mockery*] You are a pretty lover!

ROUS. Madge!

MADGE. [*Smiling*] I've heard that lovers do what their girls ask them—[JAN *sounds the cuckoo's notes*]—but that's not true, it seems!

ROUS. You'd make a blackleg of me!

MADGE. [*With her eyes half-closed*] Do it for me!

ROUS. [*Dashing his hand across his brow*] Damn! I can't!

MADGE. [*Swiftly*] Do it for me!

ROUS. [*Through his teeth*] Don't play the wanton with me!

MADGE. [*With a movement of her hand towards* JAN— *quick and low*] I'd do *that* to get the children bread!

ROUS. [*In a fierce whisper*] Madge! Oh, Madge!

MADGE. [*With soft mockery*] But *you* can't break your word with me!

ROUS. [*With a choke*] Then, Begod, I can!
[*He turns and rushes off.*

[MADGE *stands with a faint smile on her face, looking after him. She moves to the table.*

MADGE. I have done for Roberts!
[*She sees that* MRS. ROBERTS *has sunk back in her chair.*

MADGE. [*Running to her, and feeling her hands*] You're as cold as a stone! You want a drop of brandy. Jan, run to the "Lion"; say I sent you for Mrs. Roberts.

MRS. ROBERTS. [*With a feeble movement*] I'll just sit quiet, Madge. Give Jan—his—tea.

MADGE. [*Giving* JAN *a slice of bread*] There, ye little rascal. Hold your piping. [*Going to the fire, she kneels.*] It's going out.

MRS. ROBERTS. [*With a faint smile*] 'Tis all the same!
[JAN *begins to blow his whistle.*

MADGE. Tsht! Tsht!—you——   [JAN *stops.*

MRS. ROBERTS. [*Smiling*] Let 'im play, Madge.

MADGE. [*On her knees at the fire, listening*] Waiting an'
waiting. I've no patience with it; waiting an' waiting—that's
what a woman has to do! Can you hear them at it—I can!

[*She leans her elbows on the table, and her chin on her hands..
Behind her,* MRS. ROBERTS *leans forward, with painful and
growing excitement, as the sounds of the strikers' meeting come in.*

The curtain falls.

SCENE II

*It is past four. In a grey, failing light, an open muddy space is
crowded with workmen. Beyond, divided from it by a barbed-
wire fence, is the raised towing-path of a canal, on which is
moored a barge. In the distance are marshes and snow-covered
hills. The "Works'" high wall runs from the canal across the
open space, and in the angle of this wall is a rude platform of
barrels and boards. On it,* HARNESS *is standing.* ROBERTS,
*a little apart from the crowd, leans his back against the wall.
On the raised towing-path two bargemen lounge and smoke
indifferently.*

HARNESS. [*Holding out his hand*] Well, I've spoken to you
straight. If I speak till to-morrow I can't say more.

JAGO. [*A dark, sallow, Spanish-looking man, with a short, thin
beard*] Mister, want to ask you! Can they get blacklegs?

BULGIN. [*Menacing*] Let 'em try.

[*There are savage murmurs from the crowd.*

BROWN. [*A round-faced man*] Where could they get 'em then?

EVANS. [*A small restless, harassed man, with a fighting face*]
There's always blacklegs; it's the nature of 'em. There's always
men that'll save their own skins.

[*Another savage murmur. There is a movement, and old*
THOMAS, *joining the crowd, takes his stand in front.*

HARNESS. [*Holding up his hand*] They can't get them. But

that won't help you. Now, men, be reasonable. Your demands would have brought on us the burden of a dozen strikes at a time when we were not prepared for them. The Unions live by Justice, not to one, but all. Any fair man will tell you —you were ill-advised! I don't say you go too far for that which you're entitled to, but you're going too far for the moment; you've dug a pit for yourselves. Are you to stay there, or are you to climb out? Come!

LEWIS. [*A clean-cut Welshman with a dark moustache*] You've hit it, Mister! Which is it to be?

[*Another movement in the crowd, and* ROUS, *coming quickly, takes his stand next* THOMAS.

HARNESS. Cut your demands to the right pattern, and we'll see you through; refuse, and don't expect me to waste my time coming down here again. I'm not the sort that speaks at random, as you ought to know by this time. If you're the sound men I take you for—no matter who advises you against it —[*he fixes his eyes on* ROBERTS] you'll make up your minds to come in, and trust to us to get your terms. Which is it to be? Hands together, and victory—or—the starvation you've got now? [*A prolonged murmur from the crowd.*

JAGO. [*Sullenly*] Talk about what you know.

HARNESS. [*Lifting his voice above the murmur*] Know? [*With cold passion.*] All that you've been through, my friend, I've been through—I was through it when I was no bigger than [*pointing to a youth*] that shaver there; the Unions then weren't what they are now. What's made them strong? It's hands together that's made them strong. I've been through it all, I tell you, the brand's on my soul yet. I know what you've suffered—there's nothing you can tell me that I don't know; but the whole is greater than the part, and you are only the part. Stand by us, and we will stand by you.

[*Quartering them with his eyes, he waits. The murmuring swells; the men form little groups.* GREEN, BULGIN, *and* LEWIS *talk together.*

LEWIS. Speaks very sensible, the Union chap.

GREEN. [*Quietly*] Ah! if I'd a been *listened* to, you'd 'ave 'eard sense these two months past. [*The bargemen are seen laughing.*

LEWIS. [*Pointing*] Look at those two blanks over the fence there!

BULGIN. [*With gloomy violence*] They'd best stop their cackle, or I'll break their jaws.

JAGO. [*Suddenly*] You say the furnace men's paid enough?

HARNESS. I did not say they were paid enough; I said they were paid as much as the furnace men in similar works elsewhere.

EVANS. That's a lie. [*Hubbub.*] What about Harper's?

HARNESS. [*With cold irony*] You may look at home for lies, my man. Harper's shifts are longer, the pay works out the same.

HENRY ROUS. [*A dark edition of his brother George*] Will ye support us in double pay overtime Saturdays?

HARNESS. Yes, we will.

JAGO. What have ye done with our subscriptions?

HARNESS. [*Coldly*] I have told you what we *will* do with them.

EVANS. Ah! *will*, it's always will! Ye'd have our mates desert us.   [*Hubbub.*

BULGIN. [*Shouting*] Hold your row!

[*EVANS looks round angrily.*

HARNESS. [*Lifting his voice*] Those who know their right hands from their lefts know that the Unions are neither thieves nor traitors. I've said my say. Figure it out, my lads; when you want me you know where I shall be.

[*He jumps down, the crowd gives way, he passes through them, and goes away. A bargeman looks after him, jerking his pipe with a derisive gesture. The men close up in groups, and many looks are cast at ROBERTS, who stands alone against the wall.*

EVANS. He wants ye to turn blacklegs, that's what he wants. He wants ye to go back on us. Sooner than turn blackleg—I'd starve, I would.

BULGIN. Who's talkin' o' blacklegs—mind what you're saying, will you?

BLACKSMITH. [*A youth with yellow hair and huge arms*] What about the women?

EVANS. They can stand what we can stand, I suppose, can't they?

BLACKSMITH. Ye've no wife?

EVANS. An' don't want one.

THOMAS. [*Raising his voice*] Aye! Give us the power to come to terms with London, lads.

DAVIES. [*A dark, slow-fly, gloomy man*] Go up the platform, if you got anything to say, go up an' say it.

[*There are cries of "Thomas!" He is pushed towards the platform; he ascends it with difficulty, and bares his head, waiting for silence. A hush!*

RED-HAIRED YOUTH. [*Suddenly*] Coot old Thomas!

[*A hoarse laugh; the bargemen exchange remarks; a hush again, and* THOMAS *begins speaking.*

THOMAS. We are all in the tepth together, and it iss Nature that has put us there.

HENRY ROUS. It's London put us there!

EVANS. It's the Union.

THOMAS. It iss not London; nor it iss not the Union—it iss Nature. It iss no disgrace whateffer to a potty to give in to Nature. For this Nature iss a fery pig thing; it is pigger than what a man is. There iss more years to my hett than to the hett of any one here. It is fery pat, look you, this coing against Nature. It is pat to make other potties suffer, when there is nothing to pe cot py it. [*A laugh.* THOMAS *angrily goes on.*] What are ye laughing at? It is pat, I say! We are fighting for a principle; there is nopotty that shall say I am not a peliever in principle. Putt when Nature says "No further," then it is no coot snapping your fingers in her face.

[*A laugh from* ROBERTS, *and murmurs of approval.*] This Nature must pe humort. It is a man's pisiness to pe pure, honest, just and merciful. That's what Chapel tells you. [*To* ROBERTS, *angrily.*] And, look you, David Roberts, Chapel tells you ye can do that without coing against Nature.

JAGO. What about the Union?

THOMAS. I ton't trust the Union; they haf treated us like tirt. "Do what we tell you," said they. I haf peen captain of

the furnace men twenty years, and I say to the Union—
[*excitedly*]—"Can you tell me then, as well as I can tell you,
what iss the right wages for the work that these men do?" For
fife and twenty years I haf paid my moneys to the Union and—
[*with great excitement*]—for nothings! What iss that but
roguery, for all that this Mr. Harness says!   [*Murmurs.*

EVANS.   Hear, hear.

HENRY ROUS.   Get on with you! Cut on with it then!

THOMAS.   Look you, if a man toes not trust me, am I coing
to trust him?

JAGO.   That's right.

THOMAS.   Let them alone for rogues, and act for ourselves.
                                                    [*Murmurs.*

BLACKSMITH.   That's what we been doin', haven't we?

THOMAS.   [*With increased excitement*] I wass brought up to
do for meself. I wass brought up to go without a thing, if I hat
not moneys to puy it. There iss too much, look you, of doing
things with other people's moneys. We haf fought fair, and if
we haf peen beaten, it iss no fault of ours. Gif us the power to
make terms with London for ourself; if we ton't succeed, I say
it iss petter to take our peating like men, than to tie like togs, or
hang on to others' coat-tails to make them do our pusiness for us!

EVANS.   [*Muttering*] Who wants to?

THOMAS.   [*Craning*] What's that? If I stand up to a potty,
and he knocks me town, I am not to go hollering to other potties
to help me; I am to stand up again; and if he knocks me town
properly, I am to stay there, isn't that right?   [*Laughter.*

JAGO.   No Union!

HENRY ROUS.   Union!   [*Others take up the shout.*

EVANS.   Blacklegs!

          [BULGIN *and the* BLACKSMITH *shake their fists at* EVANS.

THOMAS.   [*With a gesture*] I am an old man, look you.
                    [*A sudden silence, then murmurs again.*

LEWIS.   Olt fool, with his "No Union!"

BULGIN.   Them furnace chaps! For twopence I'd smash
the faces o' the lot of them.

GREEN. If I'd 'a been listened to at the first——

THOMAS. [*Wiping his brow*] I'm comin' now to what I was coing to say——

DAVIES. [*Muttering*] An' time too!

THOMAS. [*Solemnly*] Chapel says: Ton't carry on this strike! Put an end to it!

JAGO. That's a lie! Chapel says go on!

THOMAS. [*Scornfully*] Inteet! I haf cars to my head.

RED-HAIRED YOUTH. Ah! long ones! [*A laugh.*

JAGO. Your ears have misbeled you then.

THOMAS. [*Excitedly*] Ye cannot be right if I am, ye cannot haf it both ways.

RED-HAIRED YOUTH. Chapel can though!

[*"The Shaver" laughs; there are murmurs from the crowd.*

THOMAS. [*Fixing his eyes on "The Shaver"*] Ah! ye're coing the roat to tamnation. An' so I say to all of you. If ye co against Chapel I will not pe with you, nor will any other Got-fearing man.

[*He steps down from the platform.* JAGO *makes his way towards it. There are cries of "Don't let 'im go up!"*

JAGO. Don't let him go up? That's free speech, that is. [*He goes up.*] I ain't got much to say to you. Look at the matter plain; ye've come the road this far, and now you want to chuck the journey. We've all been in one boat; and now you want to pull in two. We engineers have stood by you; ye're ready now, are ye, to give us the go-by? If we'd a-known that before, we'd not a-started out with you so early one bright morning! That's all I've got to say. Old man Thomas a'n't got his Bible lesson right. If you give up to London, or to Harness, now, it's givin' us the chuck—to save your skins—you won't get over that, my boys; it's a dirty thing to do.

[*He gets down; during his little speech, which is ironically spoken, there is a restless discomfort in the crowd.* ROUS, *stepping forward, jumps on the platform. He has an air of fierce distraction. Sullen murmurs of disapproval from the crowd.*

ROUS. [*Speaking with great excitement*] I'm no blanky orator,

mates, but wot I say is drove from me. What I say is yuman
nature. Can a man set an' see 'is mother starve? Can 'e now?

ROBERTS. [*Starting forward*] Rous!

ROUS. [*Staring at him fiercely*] Sim 'Arness said fair! I've
changed my mind.

EVANS. Ah! Turned your coat you mean!

                    [*The crowd manifests a great surprise.*

LEWIS. [*Apostrophizing* ROUS] Hallo! What's turned him
round?

ROUS. [*Speaking with intense excitement*] 'E said fair. "Stand
by us," 'e said, "and we'll stand by you." That's where we've
been makin' our mistake this long time past; and who's to blame
for't? [*He points at* ROBERTS.] That man there! "No," 'e
said, "fight the robbers," 'e said, "squeeze the breath out o'
them!" But it's not the breath out o' them that's being
squeezed; it's the breath out of *us* and *ours*, and that's the book
of truth. I'm no orator, mates, it's the flesh and blood in me
that's speakin', it's the heart o' me. [*With a menacing, yet half
ashamed movement towards* ROBERTS.] He'll speak to you
again, mark my words, but don't ye listen. [*The crowd groans.*]
It's hell fire that's on that man's tongue. [ROBERTS *is seen
laughing.*] Sim 'Arness is right. What are we without the
Union—handful o' parched leaves—a puff o' smoke. I'm no
orator, but I say: Chuck it up! Chuck it up! Sooner than go
on starving the women and the children.

[*The murmurs of acquiescence almost drown the murmurs of
dissent.*

EVANS. What's turned *you* to blacklegging?

ROUS. [*With a furious look*] Sim 'Arness knows what he's
talkin' about. Give us power to come to terms with London;
I'm no orator, but I say—have done wi' this black misery!

[*He gives his muffler a twist, jerks his head back and jumps off
the platform. The crowd applauds and surges forward. Amid
cries of "That's enough!" "Up Union!" "Up Harness!"
ROBERTS quietly ascends the platform. There is a moment of
silence.*

BLACKSMITH.   We don't want to hear you.   Shut it!

HENRY ROUS.   Get down!

[*Amid such cries they surge towards the platform.*

EVANS.   [*Fiercely*] Let 'im speak!   Roberts!   Roberts!

BULGIN.   [*Muttering*] He'd better look out that I don't crack 'is skull.

[ROBERTS *faces the crowd, probing them with his eyes till they gradually become silent. He begins speaking. One of the bargemen rises and stands.*

ROBERTS.   You don't want to hear me, then?   You'll listen to Rous and to that old man, but not to me.   You'll listen to Sim Harness of the Union that's treated you *so fair*; maybe you'll listen to those men from London?   Ah!   You groan!   What for?   You love their feet on your necks, don't you?   [*Then as* BULGIN *elbows his way towards the platform, with calm pathos.*] You'd like to break my jaw, John Bulgin.   Let me speak, then do your smashing, if it gives you pleasure.   [BULGIN *stands motionless and sullen.*]   Am I a liar, a coward, a traitor?   If only I were, ye'd listen to me, I'm sure.   [*The murmurings cease, and there is now dead silence.*]   Is there a man of you here that has less to gain by striking?   Is there a man of you that had more to lose?   Is there a man of you that has given up *eight hundred* pounds since this trouble here began?   Come now, is there?   How much has Thomas given up—ten pounds or five, or what?   You listened to him, and what had he to say?   "None can pretend," he said, "that I'm not a believer in principle—[*with biting irony*]—but when Nature says: 'No further,' 'tes going agenst Nature."   *I* tell you if a man cannot say to Nature: "Budge me from this if ye can!"—[*with a sort of exaltation*]—his principles are but his belly.   "Oh, but," Thomas says, "a man can be pure and honest, just and merciful, and take off his hat to Nature!"   *I* tell you Nature's neither pure nor honest, just nor merciful.   You chaps that live over the hill, an' go home dead beat in the dark on a snowy night— don't ye fight your way every inch of it?   Do ye go lyin' down an' trustin' to the tender mercies of this merciful Nature?   Try

it and you'll soon know with what ye've got to deal.   'Tes only
by that—[*he strikes a blow with his clenched fist*]—in Nature's
face that a man can be a man.   "Give in," says Thomas, "go
down on your knees; throw up your foolish fight, an' perhaps,"
he said, "perhaps your enemy will chuck you down a crust."

JAGO.   Never!

EVANS.   Curse them!

THOMAS.   I nefer said that.

ROBERTS.   [*Bitingly*] If ye did not say it, man, ye meant it.
An' what did ye say about Chapel?   "Chapel's against it," ye
said.   "She's against it!"   Well, if Chapel and Nature go
hand in hand, it's the first I've ever heard of it.   That young
man there—[*pointing to* ROUS]—said I 'ad 'ell fire on my tongue.
If I had I would use it all to scorch and wither this talking of
surrender.   Surrendering 's the work of cowards and traitors.

HENRY ROUS.   [*As* GEORGE ROUS *moves forward*] Go for
him, George—don't stand his lip!

ROBERTS.   [*Flinging out his finger*] Stop there, George Rous,
it's no time this to settle personal matters.   [ROUS *stops.*]   But
there was one other spoke to you—Mr. Simon Harness.   We
have not much to thank Mr. Harness and the Union for.   They
said to us "Desert your mates, or we'll desert you."   An' they
did desert us.

EVANS.   They did.

ROBERTS.   Mr. Simon Harness is a clever man, but he
has come too late.   [*With intense conviction.*]   For all that
Mr. Simon Harness says, for all that Thomas, Rous, for all
that any man present here can say—*We've won the fight!*
[*The crowd sags nearer, looking eagerly up.   With withering
scorn.*]   You've felt the pinch o't in your bellies.   You've
forgotten what that fight 'as been; many times I have told you;
I will tell you now this once again.   The fight o' the country's
body and blood against a blood-sucker.   The fight of those that
spend theirselves with every blow they strike and every breath
they draw, against a thing that fattens on them, and grows and
grows by the law of *merciful* Nature.   That thing is Capital!

A thing that buys the sweat o' men's brows, and the tortures o' their brains, at its own price. *Don't I* know that? Wasn't the work o' *my* brains bought for seven hundred pounds, and hasn't one hundred thousand pounds been gained them by that seven hundred without the stirring of a finger? It is a thing that will take as much and give you as little as it can. That's *Capital*! A thing that will say—"I'm very sorry for you, poor fellows—you have a cruel time of it, I know," but will not give one sixpence of its dividends to help you have a better time. That's Capital! Tell me, for all their talk is there one of them that will consent to another penny on the Income Tax to help the poor? That's Capital! A white-faced, stony-hearted monster! Ye have got it on its knees; are ye to give up at the last minute to save your miserable bodies pain? When I went this morning to those old men from London, I looked into their very 'earts. One of them was sitting there—Mr. Scantlebury, a mass of flesh nourished on us: sittin' there for all the world like the shareholders in this Company, that sit not moving tongue nor finger, takin' dividends—a great dumb ox that can only be roused when its food is threatened. I looked into his eyes and I saw *he was afraid*—afraid for himself and his dividends, afraid for his fees, afraid of the very shareholders he stands for; and all but one of them's afraid—like children that get into a wood at night, and start at every rustle of the leaves. I ask you, men—[*he pauses, holding out his hand till there is utter silence*]—Give me a free hand to tell them: "Go you back to London. The men have nothing for you!" [*A murmuring.*] Give me that, an' I swear to you, within a week you shall have from London all you want.

EVANS, JAGO, AND OTHERS. A free hand! Give him a free hand! Bravo—bravo!

ROBERTS. 'Tis not for this little moment of time we're fighting [*the murmuring dies*], not for ourselves, our own little bodies, and their wants, 'tis for all those that come after throughout all time. [*With intense sadness.*] Oh! men—for the love o' them, don't roll up another stone upon their heads, don't help to blacken the sky, an' let the bitter sea in over them. They're welcome to the worst that can happen to me, to the worst that can happen to us all, aren't they—aren't they? If we can shake [*passionately*] that white-faced monster with the bloody lips, that has sucked the life out of ourselves, our wives and children, since the world began. [*Dropping the note of passion, but with the utmost weight and intensity.*] If we have not the hearts of men to stand against it breast to breast, and eye to eye, and force it backward till it cry for mercy, it will go on sucking life; and we shall stay for ever what we are [*in almost a whisper*] less than the very dogs.

[*An utter stillness, and* Roberts *stands rocking his body slightly, with his eyes burning the faces of the crowd.*

Evans and Jago. [*Suddenly*] Roberts!

[*The shout is taken up.*]

[*There is a slight movement in the crowd, and* Madge *passing below the towing-path stops by the platform, looking up at* Roberts. *A sudden doubting silence.*

Roberts. "Nature," says that old man, "give in to Nature." *I* tell you, strike your blow in Nature's face—an' let it do its worst!

[*He catches sight of* Madge, *his brows contract, he looks away.*

Madge. [*In a low voice—close to the platform*] Your wife's dying!

[Roberts *glares at her as if torn from some pinnacle of exaltation.*

Roberts. [*Trying to stammer on*] I say to you—answer them—answer them——

[*He is drowned by the murmur in the crowd.*

Thomas. [*Stepping forward*] Ton't you hear her, then?

Roberts. What is it?   [*A dead silence.*

Thomas. Your wife, man!

[Roberts *hesitates, then with a gesture, he leaps down, and goes away below the towing-path, the men making way for him. The standing bargeman opens and prepares to light a lantern. Daylight is fast failing.*

MADGE.   He needn't have hurried!   Annie Roberts is dead.
[*Then in the silence, passionately.*]   You pack of blinded hounds!
How many more women are you going to let die?

[*The crowd shrinks back from her, and breaks up in groups, with
a confused, uneasy movement.   MADGE goes quickly away below
the towing-path.   There is a hush as they look after her.*

LEWIS.   There's a spitfire, for ye!

BULGIN.   [*Growling*] I'll smash 'er jaw.

GREEN.   If I'd a-been listened to, that poor woman——

THOMAS.   It's a judgment on him for coing against Chapel.
I tolt him how 'twould be!

EVANS.   All the more reason for sticking by 'im.   [*A
cheer.*]   Are you goin' to desert him now 'e's down?   Are you
goin' to chuck him over, now 'e's lost 'is wife?

[*The crowd is murmuring and cheering all at once.*

ROUS.   [*Stepping in front of platform*] Lost his wife!   Aye!
Can't ye see?   Look at home, look at your own wives!   What's
to save them?   Ye'll have the same in all your houses before
long!

LEWIS.   Aye, aye!

HENRY ROUS.   Right!   George, right!

[*There are murmurs of assent.*

ROUS.   It's not us that's blind, it's Roberts.   How long will
ye put up with 'im!

HENRY ROUS, BULGIN, DAVIES.   Give 'im the chuck!

[*The cry is taken up.*

EVANS.   [*Fiercely*] Kick a man that's down?   Down?

HENRY ROUS.   Stop his jaw there!

[EVANS *throws up his arm at a threat from* BULGIN.   *The
bargeman, who has lighted the lantern, holds it high above his head.*

ROUS.   [*Springing on to the platform*] What brought him
down then, but 'is own black obstinacy?   Are ye goin' to follow
a man that can't see better than that where he's goin'?

EVANS.   He's lost 'is wife.

ROUS.   An' whose fault's that but his own?   'Ave done
with 'im, I say, before he's killed your own wives and mothers.

DAVIES.   Down 'im!

HENRY ROUS.   He's finished!

BROWN.   We've had enough of 'im!

BLACKSMITH.   Too much!

[*The crowd takes up these cries, excepting only* EVANS, JAGO, *and* GREEN, *who is seen to argue mildly with the* BLACKSMITH.

ROUS.   [*Above the hubbub*] We'll make terms with the Union, lads.   [*Cheers.*

EVANS.   [*Fiercely*] Ye blacklegs!

BULGIN.   [*Savagely—squaring up to him*] Who are ye callin' blacklegs, Rat?

[EVANS *throws up his fists, parries the blow, and returns it. They fight.   The bargemen are seen holding up the lantern and enjoying the sight.   Old* THOMAS *steps forward and holds out his hands.*

THOMAS.   Shame on your strife!

[*The* BLACKSMITH, BROWN, LEWIS, *and the* RED-HAIRED YOUTH *pull* EVANS *and* BULGIN *apart.   The stage is almost dark.*

                    The curtain falls.

ACT III

It is five o'clock. In the UNDERWOODS' *drawing-room, which is artistically furnished,* ENID *is sitting on the sofa working at a baby's frock.* EDGAR, *by a little spindle-legged table in the centre of the room, is fingering a china-box. His eyes are fixed on the double doors that lead into the dining-room.*

EDGAR.   [*Putting down the china-box, and glancing at his watch*] Just on five, they're all in there waiting, except Frank. Where's he?

ENID.   He's had to go down to Gasgoyne's about a contract. Will you want him?

EDGAR.   He can't help us. This is a directors' job. [*Motioning towards a single door half hidden by a curtain.*] Father in his room?

ENID.   Yes.

EDGAR.   I wish he'd stay there, Enid. [ENID *looks up at him.*] This is a beastly business, old girl.

   [*He takes up the little box again and turns it over and over.*

ENID.   I went to the Roberts's this afternoon, Ted.

EDGAR.   That wasn't very wise.

ENID.   He's simply killing his wife.

EDGAR.   We are, you mean.

ENID.   [*Suddenly*] Roberts *ought* to give way!

EDGAR.   There's a lot to be said on the men's side.

ENID.   I don't feel half so sympathetic with them as I did before I went. They just set up class feeling against you. Poor Annie was looking dreadfully bad—fire going out, and nothing fit for her to eat. [EDGAR *walks to and fro.*] But she would stand up for Roberts. When you see all this wretchedness going on and feel you can do nothing, you have to shut your eyes to the whole thing.

53

EDGAR.   If you can.

ENID.   When I went I was all on their side, but as soon as I got there I began to feel quite different at once.   People talk about sympathy with the working classes, they don't know what it means to try and put it into practice.   It seems hopeless.

EDGAR.   Ah! well.

ENID.   It's dreadful going on with the men in this state.   I do hope the Dad will make concessions.

EDGAR.   He won't.   [*Gloomily.*]   It's a sort of religion with him.   Curse it!   I know what's coming!   He'll be voted down.

ENID.   They wouldn't dare!

EDGAR.   They will—they're in a funk.

ENID.   [*Indignantly*] He'd never stand it!

EDGAR.   [*With a shrug*] My dear girl, if you're beaten in a vote, you've got to stand it.

ENID.   Oh! [*She gets up in alarm.*]   But would he resign?

EDGAR.   Of course!   It goes to the roots of his beliefs.

ENID.   But he's so *wrapped up in this company*, Ted! There'd be nothing left for him!   It'd be dreadful!   [EDGAR *shrugs his shoulders.*]   Oh, Ted, he's so old now!   You mustn't let them!

EDGAR.   [*Hiding his feelings in an outburst*] My sympathies in this strike are all on the side of the men.

ENID.   He's been Chairman for more than thirty years! He made the whole thing!   And think of the bad times they've had, it's always been he who pulled them through.   Oh, Ted, you must——

EDGAR.   What is it you want?   You said just now you hoped he'd make concessions.   Now you want me to back him in not making them.   This isn't a game, Enid!

ENID.   [*Hotly*] It isn't a game to *me* that the Dad's in danger of losing all he cares about in life.   If he won't give way, and he's beaten, it'll simply break him down!

EDGAR.   Didn't you say it was dreadful going on with the men in this state?

ENID.   But can't you see, Ted, Father'll never get over it!

You must stop them somehow.   The others are afraid of him.
If you back him up——

EDGAR.   [*Putting his hand to his head*] Against my con-
victions—against yours!   The moment it begins to pinch one
personally——

ENID.   It isn't personal, it's the Dad!

EDGAR.   Your family or yourself, and over goes the show!

ENID.   [*Resentfully*] If you don't take it seriously, I do.

EDGAR.   I am as fond of him as you are; that's nothing to
do with it.

ENID.   We can't tell about the men; it's all guess-work.
But we know the Dad might have a stroke any day.   D'you
mean to say that he isn't more to you than——

EDGAR.   Of course he is.

ENID.   I don't understand you then.

EDGAR.   H'm!

ENID.   If it were for oneself it would be different, but for
our own Father!   You don't seem to realize.

EDGAR.   I realize perfectly.

ENID.   It's your first duty to save him.

EDGAR.   I wonder.

ENID.   [*Imploring*] Oh, Ted!   It's the only interest he's got
left; it'll be like a death-blow to him!

EDGAR.   [*Restraining his emotion*] I know.

ENID.   Promise!

EDGAR.   I'll do what I can.   [*He turns to the double doors.*
[*The curtained door is opened, and* ANTHONY *appears.*
EDGAR *opens the double doors, and passes through.*

[SCANTLEBURY'S *voice is faintly heard:* "*Past five; we shall
never get through—have to eat another dinner at that hotel!*"
The doors are shut. ANTHONY *walks forward.*

ANTHONY.   You've been seeing Roberts, I hear.

ENID.   Yes.

ANTHONY.   Do you know what trying to bridge such a gulf
as this is like?   [ENID *puts her work on the little table, and
faces him.*]   Filling a sieve with sand!

Enid.   Don't!

Anthony.   You think with your gloved hands you can cure
the trouble of the century.   [*He passes on.*

Enid.   Father! [Anthony *stops at the double doors.*]   I'm
only thinking of you!

Anthony.   [*More softly*] I can take care of myself, my dear.

Enid.   Have you thought what'll happen if you're beaten
—[*she points*]—in there?

Anthony.   I don't mean to be.

Enid.   Oh! Father, don't give them a chance.   You're
not well; need you go to the meeting at all?

Anthony.   [*With a grim smile*] Cut and run?

Enid.   But they'll outvote you!

Anthony.   [*Putting his hand on the doors*] We shall see!

Enid.   I beg you, Dad!   [Anthony *looks at her softly.*]
Won't you? [Anthony *shakes his head. He opens the doors.
A buzz of voices comes in.*

Scantlebury.   Can one get dinner on that 6.30 train up?

Tench.   No, sir, I believe not, sir.

Wilder.   Well, I shall speak out; I've had enough of this.

Edgar.   [*Sharply*] What?

[*It ceases instantly.* Anthony *passes through, closing the
doors behind him.* Enid *springs to them with a gesture of dismay.
She puts her hand on the knob, and begins turning it; then goes to
the fireplace, and taps her foot on the fender.   Suddenly she rings
the bell.* Frost *comes in by the door that leads into the hall.*

Frost.   Yes, M'm?

Enid.   When the men come, Frost, please show them in
here; the hall's cold.

Frost.   I could put them in the pantry, M'm.

Enid.   No. I don't want to—to offend them; they're so
touchy.

Frost.   Yes, M'm. [*Pause.*]   Excuse me, Mr. Anthony's
'ad nothing to eat all day.

Enid.   I know, Frost.

Frost.   Nothin' but two whiskies and sodas, M'm.

ENID. Oh! you oughtn't to have let him have those.

FROST. [*Gravely*] Mr. Anthony is a little difficult, M'm. It's not as if he were a younger man, an' knew what was good for 'im; he will have his own way.

ENID. I suppose we all want that.

FROST. Yes, M'm. [*Quietly.*] Excuse me speakin' about the strike. I'm sure if the other gentlemen were to give up to Mr. Anthony, and quietly let the men 'ave what they want, afterwards, that'd be the best way. I find that very useful with him at times, M'm. [ENID *shakes her head.*] If he's crossed, it makes him violent [*with an air of discovery*], and I've noticed in my own case, when I'm violent I'm always sorry for it afterwards.

ENID. [*With a smile*] Are *you* ever violent, Frost?

FROST. Yes, M'm; oh! sometimes very violent.

ENID. I've never seen you.

FROST. [*Impersonally*] No, M'm; that is so.

[ENID *fidgets towards the door's back.*]
[*With feeling.*] Bein' with Mr. Anthony, as you know, M'm, ever since I was fifteen, it worries me to see him crossed like this at his age. I've taken the liberty to speak to Mr. Wanklin [*dropping his voice*]—seems to be the most sensible of the gentlemen—but 'e said to me: "That's all very well, Frost, but this strike's a very serious thing," 'e said. "Serious for all parties, no doubt," I said, "but yumour 'im, sir," I said, "yumour 'im. It's like this, if a man comes to a stone wall, 'e doesn't drive 'is 'ead against it, 'e gets over it." "Yes," 'e said, "you'd better tell your master that." [FROST *looks at his nails.*] That's where it is, M'm. I said to Mr. Anthony this morning: "Is it worth it, sir?" "Damn it," he said to me, "Frost! Mind your own business, or take a month's notice!" Beg pardon, M'm, for using such a word.

ENID. [*Moving to the double doors, and listening*] Do you know that man Roberts, Frost?

FROST. Yes, M'm; that's to say, not to speak to. But to *look* at 'im you can tell what *he's* like.

ENID. [*Stopping*] Yes?

FROST. He's not one of these 'ere ordinary 'armless Socialists. 'E's violent; got a fire inside 'im. What I call "personal." A man may 'ave what opinion 'e likes, so long as 'e's not personal; when 'e's that 'e's *not* safe.

ENID. I think that's what my Father feels about Roberts.

FROST. No doubt, M'm, Mr. Anthony has a feeling against him. [ENID *glances at him sharply, but finding him in perfect earnest, stands biting her lips, and looking at the double doors.*] It's a regular right down struggle between the two. I've no patience with this Roberts; from what I 'ear he's just an ordinary workin' man like the rest of 'em. If he did invent a thing he's no worse off than 'undreds of others. My brother invented a new kind o' dumb waiter—nobody gave *him* anything for it, an' there it is, bein' used all over the place. [ENID *moves closer to the double doors.*] There's a kind o' man that never forgives the world, because 'e wasn't born a gentleman. What I say is—no man that's a gentleman looks down on another man because 'e 'appens to be a class or two above 'im, no more than if 'e 'appens to be a class or two below.

ENID. [*With slight impatience*] Yes, I know, Frost, of course. Will you please go in and ask if they'll have some tea; say I sent you.

FROST. Yes, M'm. [*He opens the doors gently and goes in. There is a momentary sound of earnest, rather angry talk.*

WILDER. I don't agree with you.

WANKLIN. We've had this over a dozen times.

EDGAR. [*Impatiently*] Well, what's the proposition?

SCANTLEBURY. Yes, what does your Father say? Tea? Not for me, not for me!

WANKLIN. What I understand the Chairman to say is this—— [FROST *re-enters, closing the door behind him.*

ENID. [*Moving from the door*] Won't they have any tea, Frost? [*She goes to the little table, and remains motionless, looking at the baby's frock.* [*A parlourmaid enters from the hall.*

PARLOURMAID. A Miss Thomas, M'm.

ENID. [*Raising her head*] Thomas? What Miss Thomas
—d'you mean a——?

PARLOURMAID. Yes, M'm.

ENID. [*Blankly*] Oh! Where is she?

PARLOURMAID. In the porch.

ENID. I don't want—— [*She hesitates.*]

FROST. Shall I dispose of her, M'm?

ENID. I'll come out. No, show her in here, Ellen.

[*The* PARLOURMAID *and* FROST *go out.* ENID *pursing her
lips, sits at the little table, taking up the baby's frock. The*
PARLOURMAID *ushers in* MADGE THOMAS *and goes out;*
MADGE *stands by the door.*

ENID. Come in. What is it? What have you come for,
please?

MADGE. Brought a message from Mrs. Roberts.

ENID. A message? Yes.

MADGE. She asks you to look after her Mother.

ENID. I don't understand.

MADGE. [*Sullenly*] That's the message.

ENID. But—what—why?

MADGE. Annie Roberts is dead. [*There is a silence.*

ENID. [*Horrified*] But it's only a little more than an hour
since I saw her.

MADGE. Of cold and hunger.

ENID. [*Rising*] Oh! that's not true! the poor thing's
heart—— What makes you look at me like that? I tried to
help her.

MADGE. [*With suppressed savagery*] I thought you'd like
to know.

ENID. [*Passionately*] It's so unjust! Can't you see that I
want to help you all?

MADGE. I never harmed anyone that hadn't harmed me
first.

ENID. [*Coldly*] What harm have I done you? Why do
you speak to me like that?

MADGE. [*With the bitterest intensity*] You come out of your comfort to spy on us! A week of hunger, that's what *you* want!

Enid. [*Standing her ground*] Don't talk nonsense!

Madge. I saw her die; her hands were blue with the cold.

Enid. [*With a movement of grief*] Oh! why wouldn't she let me help her? It's such senseless pride!

Madge. Pride's better than nothing to keep your body warm.

Enid. [*Passionately*] I won't talk to you! How can you tell what I feel? It's not my fault that I was born better off than you.

Madge. We don't want your money.

Enid. You don't understand, and you don't want to; please to go away!

Madge. [*Balefully*] You've killed her, for all your soft words, you and your father——

Enid. [*With rage and emotion*] That's wicked! My father is suffering himself through this wretched strike.

Madge. [*With sombre triumph*] Then tell him Mrs. Roberts is dead! That'll make him better.

Enid. Go away!

Madge. When a person hurts us we get it back on them.

[*She makes a sudden and swift movement towards* Enid, *fixing her eyes on the child's frock lying across the little table.* Enid *snatches the frock up, as though it were the child itself. They stand a yard apart, crossing glances.*

Madge. [*Pointing to the frock with a little smile*] Ah! You felt *that*! Lucky it's her mother—not her children—you've to look after, isn't it. *She* won't trouble you long!

Enid. Go away!

Madge. I've given you the message.

[*She turns and goes out into the hall.* Enid, *motionless till she has gone, sinks down at the table, bending her head over the frock, which she is still clutching to her. The double doors are opened, and* Anthony *comes slowly in; he passes his daughter, and lowers himself into an armchair. He is very flushed.*

Enid. [*Hiding her emotion—anxiously*] What is it, Dad? [Anthony *makes a gesture, but does not speak.*] Who was it?

[ANTHONY *does not answer.* ENID *going to the double doors meets* EDGAR *coming in. They speak together in low tones.*] What is it, Ted?

EDGAR. That fellow Wilder! Taken to personalities! He was downright insulting.

ENID. What did he *say*?

EDGAR. Said, Father was too old and feeble to know what he was doing! The Dad's worth six of him!

ENID. Of course he is. [*They look at* ANTHONY.

[*The doors open wider,* WANKLIN *appears with* SCANTLEBURY.

SCANTLEBURY. [*Sotto voce*] I don't like the look of this!

WANKLIN. [*Going forward*] Come, Chairman! Wilder sends you his apologies. A man can't do more.

[WILDER, *followed by* TENCH, *comes in, and goes to* ANTHONY.

WILDER. [*Glumly*] I withdraw my words, sir. I'm sorry.

[ANTHONY *nods to him.*

ENID. You haven't come to a decision, Mr. Wanklin?

[WANKLIN *shakes his head.*

WANKLIN. We're all here, Chairman; what do you say? Shall we get on with the business, or shall we go back to the other room?

SCANTLEBURY. Yes, yes; let's get on. We must settle something. [*He turns from a small chair, and settles himself suddenly in the largest chair, with a sigh of comfort.*

[WILDER *and* WANKLIN *also sit; and* TENCH, *drawing up a straight-backed chair close to his Chairman, sits on the edge of it with the minute-book and a stylographic pen.*

ENID. [*Whispering*] I want to speak to you a minute, Ted.

[*They go out through the double doors.*

WANKLIN. Really, Chairman, it's no use soothing ourselves with a sense of false security. If this strike's not brought to an end before the General Meeting, the shareholders will certainly haul us over the coals.

SCANTLEBURY. [*Stirring*] What—what's that?

WANKLIN. I know it for a fact.

ANTHONY. Let them!

WILDER.   And get turned out?

WANKLIN.   [*To* ANTHONY] I don't mind martyrdom for a policy in which I believe, but I object to being burnt for someone else's principles.

SCANTLEBURY.   Very reasonable—you must see that, Chairman.

ANTHONY.   We owe it to other employers to stand firm.

WANKLIN.   There's a limit to that.

ANTHONY.   You were all full of fight at the start.

SCANTLEBURY.   [*With a sort of groan*] We thought the men would give in, but they—haven't!

ANTHONY.   They will!

WILDER.   [*Rising and pacing up and down*] I can't have my reputation as a man of business destroyed for the satisfaction of starving the men out.   [*Almost in tears.*]   I can't have it! How can we meet the shareholders with things in the state they are?

SCANTLEBURY.   Hear, hear—hear, hear!

WILDER.   [*Lashing himself*] If anyone expects me to say to them I've lost you fifty thousand pounds and sooner than put my pride in my pocket I'll lose you another—— [*Glancing at* ANTHONY.] It's—it's unnatural! *I don't want to* go against you, sir——

WANKLIN.   [*Persuasively*] Come, Chairman, we're *not* free agents.   We're part of a machine.   Our only business is to see the Company earns as much profit as it safely can.   If you blame me for want of principle: I say that we're Trustees. Reason tells us we shall never get back in the saving of wages what we shall lose if we continue this struggle—really, Chairman, we *must* bring it to an end, on the best terms we can make.

ANTHONY.   No!   [*There is a pause of general dismay.*]

WILDER.   It's a deadlock then.   [*Letting his hands drop with a sort of despair.*]   Now I shall never get off to Spain!

WANKLIN.   [*Retaining a trace of irony*] You hear the consequences of your victory, Chairman?

WILDER.   [*With a burst of feeling*] My wife's *ill*!

SCANTLEBURY.   Dear, dear!   You don't say so!

WILDER. If I don't get her out of this cold, I won't answer for the consequences.

[*Through the double doors* EDGAR *comes in looking very grave.*

EDGAR. [*To his Father*] Have you heard this, sir? Mrs. Roberts is dead! [*Everyone stares at him, as if trying to gauge the importance of this news.*] Enid saw her this afternoon, she had no coals, or food, or anything. It's enough!

[*There is a silence, everyone avoiding the other's eyes, except* ANTHONY, *who stares hard at his son.*

SCANTLEBURY. You don't suggest that we could have helped the poor thing?

WILDER. [*Flustered*] The woman was in bad health. Nobody can say there's any responsibility on us. At least—not on me.

EDGAR. [*Hotly*] I say that we *are* responsible.

ANTHONY. War is war!

EDGAR. Not on women!

WANKLIN. It not infrequently happens that women are the greatest sufferers.

EDGAR. If we knew that, all the more responsibility rests on us.

ANTHONY. This is no matter for amateurs.

EDGAR. Call me what you like, sir. It's sickened me. We had no right to carry things to such a length.

WILDER. I don't like this business a bit—that Radical rag will twist it to their own ends; see if they don't! They'll get up some cock-and-bull story about the poor woman's dying from starvation. I wash my hands of it.

EDGAR. You can't. None of us can.

SCANTLEBURY. [*Striking his fist on the arm of his chair*] But I protest against this——

EDGAR. Protest as you like, Mr. Scantlebury, it won't alter facts.

ANTHONY. That's enough.

EDGAR. [*Facing him angrily*] No, sir. I tell you exactly what I think. If we pretend the men are not suffering, it's humbug; and if they're suffering, we know enough of human nature to know the women are suffering more, and as to the children —well—it's damnable!   [SCANTLEBURY *rises from his chair*.] I don't say that we meant to be cruel, I don't say anything of the sort; but I do say it's criminal to shut our eyes to the facts. We employ these men, and we can't get out of it.   I don't care so much about the men, but I'd sooner resign my position on the Board than go on starving women in this way.

[*All except* ANTHONY *are now upon their feet*, ANTHONY *sits grasping the arms of his chair and staring at his son*.

SCANTLEBURY.   I don't—I don't like the way you're putting it, young sir.

WANKLIN.   You're rather overshooting the mark.

WILDER.   I should think so indeed!

EDGAR.   [*Losing control*] It's no use blinking things! If *you* want to have the death of women on your hands—*I* don't!

SCANTLEBURY.   Now, now, young man!

WILDER.   On *our* hands? Not on *mine*, I won't have it!

EDGAR.   We are five members of this Board; if we were four against it, why did we let it drift till it came to this?   You know perfectly well why—because we hoped we should starve the men out.   Well, all we've done is to starve one woman out!

SCANTLEBURY.   [*Almost hysterically*] I protest, I protest! I'm a humane man—we're all humane men!

EDGAR.   [*Scornfully*] There's nothing wrong with our *humanity*.   It's our imaginations, Mr. Scantlebury.

WILDER.   Nonsense!   My imagination's as good as yours.

EDGAR.   If so, it isn't good enough.

WILDER.   I foresaw this!

EDGAR.   Then why didn't you put your foot down?

WILDER.   Much good that would have done.

[*He looks at* ANTHONY.

EDGAR.   If you, and I, and each one of us here who say that our imaginations are so good——

SCANTLEBURY.   [*Flurried*] I never said so.

EDGAR.   [*Paying no attention*] ——had put our feet down,

the thing would have been ended long ago, and this poor woman's life wouldn't have been crushed out of her like this.   For all we can tell there may be a dozen other starving women.

SCANTLEBURY.   For God's sake, sir, don't use that word at a—at a Board meeting; it's—it's monstrous.

EDGAR.   I *will* use it, Mr. Scantlebury.

SCANTLEBURY.   Then I shall not listen to you.   I shall not listen!   It's painful to me.   [*He covers his ears.*

WANKLIN.   None of us are opposed to a settlement, except your Father.

EDGAR.   I'm certain that if the shareholders knew——

WANKLIN.   I don't think you'll find their imaginations are any better than ours.   Because a woman happens to have a weak heart——

EDGAR.   A struggle like this finds out the weak spots in everybody.   Any child knows that.   If it hadn't been for this cut-throat policy, she needn't have died like this; and there wouldn't be all this misery that anyone who isn't a fool can see is going on.   [*Throughout the foregoing* ANTHONY *has eyed his son; he now moves as though to rise, but stops as* EDGAR *speaks again.*]   I don't defend the men, or myself, or anybody.

WANKLIN.   You may have to!   A coroner's jury of dis-interested sympathizers may say some very nasty things.   We mustn't lose sight of our position.

SCANTLEBURY.   [*Without uncovering his ears*] Coroner's jury!   No, no, it's not a case for that?

EDGAR.   I've had enough of cowardice.

WANKLIN.   Cowardice is an unpleasant word, Mr. Edgar Anthony.   It will look very like cowardice if we suddenly concede the men's demands when a thing like this happens; we must be careful!

WILDER.   Of course we must.   We've no knowledge of this matter, except a rumour.   The proper course is to put the whole thing into the hands of Harness to settle for us; that's natural, that's what we *should* have come to any way.

SCANTLEBURY.   [*With dignity*] Exactly!   [*Turning to

EDGAR.] And as to you, young sir, I can't sufficiently express my—my distaste for the way you've treated the whole matter. You ought to withdraw! Talking of starvation, talking of cowardice! Considering what our views are! Except your own Father—we're all agreed the only policy is—is one of goodwill—it's most irregular, it's most improper, and all I can say is it's—it's given me pain——

     [He places his hand on the centre of his scheme.

 EDGAR. *[Stubbornly]* I withdraw nothing.

[He is about to say more when SCANTLEBURY *once more covers up his ears.* TENCH *suddenly makes a demonstration with the minute-book. A sense of having been engaged in the unusual comes over all of them, and one by one they resume their seats.* EDGAR *alone remains on his feet.*

 WILDER. *[With an air of trying to wipe something out]* I pay no attention to what young Mr. Anthony has said. Coroner's Jury! The idea's preposterous. I—I move this amendment to the Chairman's Motion: That the dispute be placed at once in the hands of Mr. Simon Harness for settlement, on the lines indicated by him this morning. Anyone second that?

         [TENCH writes in the book.

 WANKLIN. I do.

 WILDER. Very well, then; I ask the Chairman to put it to the Board.

 ANTHONY. *[With a great sigh—slowly]* We have been made the subject of an attack. *[Looking round at* WILDER *and* SCANTLEBURY *with ironical contempt.]* I take it on *my* shoulders. I am seventy-six years old. I have been Chairman of this Company since its inception two-and-thirty years ago. I have seen it pass through good and evil report. My connection with it began in the year that this young man was born. *[*EDGAR *bows his head.* ANTHONY, *gripping his chair, goes on.]* I have had to do with "men" for fifty years; I've always stood up to them; I have never been beaten yet. I have fought the men of this Company four times, and four times I have beaten them. It has been said that I am not the man I was. *[He looks* *at* WILDER.] However that may be, I am man enough to stand to my guns.

[*His voice grows stronger. The double doors are opened.* ENID *slips in, followed by* UNDERWOOD, *who restrains her.*] The men have been treated justly, they have had fair wages, we have always been ready to listen to complaints. It has been said that times have changed; if they have, I have not changed with them. Neither will I. It has been said that masters and men are equal! Cant! There can only be one master in a house! Where two men meet the better man will rule. It has been said that Capital and Labour have the same interests. Cant! Their interests are as wide asunder as the poles. It has been said that the Board is only part of a machine. Cant! We *are* the machine; its brains and sinews; it is for us to lead and to determine what is to be done, and to do it without fear or favour. Fear of the men! Fear of the shareholders! Fear of our own shadows! Before I am like that, I hope to die. [*He pauses, and meeting his son's eyes, goes on.*] There is only one way of treating "men"—with *the iron hand*. This half-and-half business, the half-and-half manners of this generation has brought all this upon us. Sentiment and softness, and what this young man, no doubt, would call his social policy. You can't eat cake and have it! This middle-class sentiment, or socialism, or whatever it may be, is rotten. Masters are masters, men are men! Yield one demand, and they will make it six. They are [*he smiles grimly*] like Oliver Twist, asking for more. If I were in *their* place I should be the same. But I am not in their place. Mark my words: one fine morning, when you have given way here, and given way there—you will find you have parted with the ground beneath your feet, and are deep in the bog of bankruptcy; and with you, floundering in that bog, will be the very men you have given way to. I have been accused of being a domineering tyrant, thinking only of my pride—I am thinking of the future of this country, threatened with the black waters of confusion, threatened with mob government, threatened with what I cannot see. If by any conduct of mine I help to bring this on us, I shall be ashamed to look my fellows in the face.

[ANTHONY *stares before him, at what he cannot see, and there is perfect stillness.* FROST *comes in from the hall, and all but* ANTHONY *look round at him uneasily.*

FROST. [*To his master*] The men are here, sir. [ANTHONY *makes a gesture of dismissal.*] Shall I bring them in, sir?

ANTHONY. Wait! [FROST *goes out,* ANTHONY *turns to face his son.*] I come to the attack that has been made upon me. [EDGAR, *with a gesture of deprecation, remains motionless with his head a little bowed.*] A woman has died. I am told that her blood is on my hands; I am told that on my hands is the starvation and the suffering of other women and children.

EDGAR. I said "on *our* hands," sir.

ANTHONY. It is the same. [*His voice grows stronger and stronger, his feeling is more and more made manifest.*] I am not aware that if my adversary suffer in a fair fight not sought by me, it is *my* fault. If I fall under *his* feet—as fall I may—I shall not complain. That will be *my* look-out—and this is —his. I cannot separate, as I would, these men from their women and children. A fair fight is a fair fight! Let them learn to think before they pick a quarrel!

EDGAR. [*In a low voice*] But is it a fair fight, Father? Look at them, and look at us! They've only this one weapon!

ANTHONY. [*Grimly*] And you're weak-kneed enough to teach them how to use it! It seems the fashion nowadays for men to take their enemy's side. I have not learnt that art. Is it my fault that they quarrelled with their Union too?

EDGAR. There is such a thing as Mercy.

ANTHONY. And Justice comes before it.

EDGAR. What seems just to one man, sir, is injustice to another.

ANTHONY. [*With suppressed passion*] You accuse me of injustice—of what amounts to inhumanity—of cruelty——

[EDGAR *makes a gesture of horror—a general frightened movement.*

WANKLIN. Come, come, Chairman!

ANTHONY. [*In a grim voice*] These are the words of my own son. They are the words of a generation that I don't understand; the words of a soft breed.

[*A general murmur. With a violent effort* ANTHONY *recovers his control.*

EDGAR. [*Quietly*] I said it of *myself*, too, Father.

[*A long look is exchanged between them, and* ANTHONY *puts out his hand with a gesture as if to sweep the personalities away; then places it against his brow, swaying as though from giddiness. There is a movement towards him. He waves them back.*

ANTHONY. Before I put this amendment to the Board, I have one more word to say. [*He looks from face to face.*] If it is carried, it means that we shall fail in what we set ourselves to do. It means that we shall fail in the duty that we owe to all Capital. It means that we shall fail in the duty that we owe ourselves. It means that we shall be open to constant attack to which we as constantly shall have to yield. Be under no misapprehension—run this time, and you will never make a stand again! You will have to fly like curs before the whips of your own men. If that is the lot you wish for, you will vote for this amendment. [*He looks again from face to face, finally resting his gaze on* EDGAR; *all sit with their eyes on the ground.* ANTHONY *makes a gesture, and* TENCH *hands him the book. He reads.*] "Moved by Mr. Wilder, and seconded by Mr. Wanklin. 'That the men's demands be placed at once in the hands of Mr. Simon Harness for settlement on the lines indicated by him this morning.'" [*With sudden vigour.*] Those in favour: Signify the same in the usual way!

[*For a minute no one moves; then hastily, just as* ANTHONY *is about to speak,* WILDER'S *hand and* WANKLIN'S *are held up, then* SCANTLEBURY'S, *and last* EDGAR'S, *who does not lift his head.*] Contrary? [ANTHONY *lifts his own hand.* [*In a clear voice.*] The amendment is carried. I resign my position on this Board.

[ENID *gasps, and there is a dead silence.* ANTHONY *sits*

motionless, his head slowly drooping; suddenly he heaves as though the whole of his life had risen up within him.] Fifty years! You have disgraced me, gentlemen. Bring in the men!

[*He sits motionless, staring before him. The Board draws hurriedly together, and forms a group.* TENCH *in a frightened manner speaks into the hall.* UNDERWOOD *almost forces* ENID *from the room.*

WILDER. [*Hurriedly*] What's to be said to them? Why isn't Harness here? Ought we to see the men before he comes? I don't——

TENCH. Will you come in, please?

[*Enter* THOMAS, GREEN, BULGIN *and* ROUS, *who file up in a row past the little table.* TENCH *sits down and writes. All eyes are fixed on* ANTHONY, *who makes no sign.*

WANKLIN. [*Stepping up to the little table, with nervous cordiality*] Well, Thomas, how's it to be? What's the result of your meeting?

ROUS. Sim Harness has our answer. He'll tell you what it is. We're waiting for him. He'll speak for us.

WANKLIN. Is that so, Thomas?

THOMAS. [*Sullenly*] Yes. Roberts will not be coming, his wife is dead.

SCANTLEBURY. Yes, yes! Poor woman! Yes! Yes!

FROST. [*Entering from the hall*] Mr. Harness, sir!

[*As* HARNESS *enters he retires.*

[HARNESS *has a piece of paper in his hand, he bows to the Directors, nods towards the men, and takes his stand behind the little table in the very centre of the room.*

HARNESS. Good evening, gentlemen.

[TENCH, *with the paper he has been writing, joins him, they speak together in low tones.*

WILDER. We've been waiting for you, Harness. Hope we shall come to some——

FROST. [*Entering from the hall*] Roberts.   [*He goes.*

[ROBERTS *comes hastily in, and stands staring at* ANTHONY. *His face is drawn and old.*

ROBERTS. Mr. Anthony, I am afraid I am a little late. I would have been here in time but for something that—has happened. [*To the men*] Has anything been said?

THOMAS. No! But, man, what made ye come?

ROBERTS. Ye told us this morning, gentlemen, to go away and reconsider our position. We have reconsidered it; we are here to bring you the men's answer. [*To* ANTHONY] Go ye back to London. We have nothing for you. By no jot or tittle do we abate our demands, nor will we until the whole of those demands are yielded.

[ANTHONY *looks at him but does not speak. There is a movement amongst the men as though they were bewildered.*

HARNESS. Roberts!

ROBERTS. [*Glancing fiercely at him, and back to* ANTHONY] Is that clear enough for ye? Is it short enough and to the point? Ye made a mistake to think that we would come to heel. Ye may break the body, but ye cannot break the spirit. Get back to London, the men have nothing for ye?

[*Pausing uneasily he takes a step towards the unmoving* ANTHONY.

EDGAR. We're all sorry for you, Roberts, but——

ROBERTS. Keep your sorrow, young man. Let your Father speak!

HARNESS. [*With the sheet of paper in his hand, speaking from behind the little table*] Roberts!

ROBERTS. [*To* ANTHONY, *with passionate intensity*] Why don't ye answer?

HARNESS. Roberts!

ROBERTS. [*Turning sharply*] What is it?

HARNESS. [*Gravely*] You're talking without the book; things have travelled past you. [*He makes a sign to* TENCH, *who beckons the Directors. They quickly sign his copy of the terms.*] Look at this, man! [*Holding up his sheet of paper.*] 'Demands conceded, *with the exception of those relating to the engineers and furnace men. Double wages for Saturday's over-time. Night-shifts as they are.*' These terms have been agreed.

The men go back to work again to-morrow.   The strike is at an end.

ROBERTS.   [*Reading the paper, and turning on the men.   They shrink back from him, all but* ROUS, *who stands his ground.   With deadly stillness*] Ye have gone back on me?   I stood by ye to the death; ye waited for *that* to throw me over!

[*The men answer, all speaking together.*

ROUS.   It's a lie!

THOMAS.   Ye were past endurance, man.

GREEN.   If ye'd listen to me——

BULGIN.   [*Under his breath*] Hold your jaw!

ROBERTS.   Ye waited for *that*!

HARNESS.   [*Taking the Directors' copy of the terms, and handing his own to* TENCH] That's enough, men.   You had better go.

[*The men shuffle slowly, awkwardly away.*

WILDER.   [*In a low, nervous voice*] There's nothing to stay for now, I suppose.   [*He follows to the door.*]   I shall have a try for that train!   Coming, Scantlebury?

SCANTLEBURY.   [*Following with* WANKLIN] Yes, yes;   wait for me.   [*He stops as* ROBERTS *speaks.*

ROBERTS.   [*To* ANTHONY] But *ye* have not signed them terms!   They can't make terms without their Chairman!   Ye would never sign them terms!

[ANTHONY *looks at him without speaking.*] Don't tell me ye have!   for the love o' God!   [*With passionate appeal*] I reckoned on ye!

HARNESS.   [*Holding out the Directors' copy of the terms*] The Board has signed!

[ROBERTS *looks dully at the signatures—dashes the paper from him, and covers up his eyes.*

SCANTLEBURY.   [*Behind his hand to* TENCH] Look after the Chairman!   He's not well;   he's not well—he had no lunch. If there's any fund started for the women and children, put me down for—for twenty pounds.

[*He goes out into the hall, in cumbrous haste;   and* WANKLIN, *who has been staring at* ROBERTS *and* ANTHONY *with twitchings of his face, follows.* EDGAR *remains seated on the sofa, looking at the ground;* TENCH, *returning to the bureau, writes in his minute-book.* HARNESS *stands by the little table, gravely watching* ROBERTS.

ROBERTS. Then you're no longer Chairman of this Company! [*Breaking into half-mad laughter.*] Ah! ha—ah, ha, ha! They've thrown ye over—thrown over their Chairman: Ah—ha—ha! [*With a sudden dreadful calm*] So—they've done us both down, Mr. Anthony?

[ENID, *hurrying through the double doors, comes quickly to her father and bends over him.*

HARNESS. [*Coming down and laying his hands on* ROBERTS' *sleeve*] For shame, Roberts! Go home quietly, man; go home!

ROBERTS. [*Tearing his arm away*] Home? [*Shrinking together—in a whisper*] Home!

ENID. [*Quietly to her father*] Come away, dear! Come to your room!

[ANTHONY *rises with an effort. He turns to* ROBERTS, *who looks at him. They stand several seconds, gazing at each other fixedly;* ANTHONY *lifts his hand, as though to salute, but lets it fall. The expression of* ROBERTS' *face changes from hostility to wonder. They bend their heads in token of respect.* ANTHONY *turns, and slowly walks towards the curtained door. Suddenly he sways as though about to fall, recovers himself and is assisted out by* ENID *and* EDGAR, *who has hurried across the room.* ROBERTS *remains motionless for several seconds, staring intently after* ANTHONY, *then goes out into the hall.*

TENCH. [*Approaching* HARNESS] It's a great weight off my mind, Mr. Harness! But what a painful scene, sir!

[*He wipes his brow.*

[HARNESS, *pale and resolute, regards with a grim half-smile the quavering* TENCH.] It's all been so violent! What did he mean by: "Done us both down?" If he has lost his wife, poor fellow, he oughtn't to have spoken to the Chairman like that!

HARNESS. A woman dead; and the two best men both broken! [UNDERWOOD *enters suddenly.*

TENCH. [*Staring at* HARNESS—*suddenly excited*] D'you know, sir—these terms, they're the *very same* we drew up together, you and I, and put to both sides before the fight began? All this—all this—and—and what for?

HARNESS. [*In a slow grim voice*] That's where the fun comes in!

[UNDERWOOD *without turning from the door makes a gesture of assent.*

The curtain falls.

JOHN GALSWORTHY

1867—1933

In John Galsworthy's earlier years no one could possibly have seen in him a world-famous author or indeed any kind of writer at all. Yet he became one of the most outstanding English novelists and dramatists of his time, and received the highest national and international honours. Moreover there was nothing vulgar in his remarkable success story, for he remained all his life unself-seeking, modest and generous, a humane influence in British and international affairs.

John Galsworthy (he pronounced it *Gollsworthy*) was born at Kingston, near London, on August 14th, 1867, the son of a wealthy London solicitor and property owner, the original of Old Jolyon in *The Forsyte Saga*, whose ancestors were small farmers in Devonshire. John was educated at Harrow, one of the most famous and exclusive of English public schools, where he was Captain of Football, and at New College, Oxford, where he studied law. He went on to Lincoln's Inn, one of the ancient legal societies in London which maintain the standards of legal qualifications and conduct, and in 1890 he was called to the Bar, that is, he qualified as a barrister, who could conduct cases in the higher courts of law. He had no need to earn his living and he never practised law, but no doubt the legal training strengthened his natural tendency to judicious impartiality of mind and precision in the use of words. It is equally significant that he was born and grew up in the nineteenth century heyday of British prosperity, when the progress of civilization seemed assured and such barbarous catastrophes as the two world wars were unthinkable. John Galsworthy, a well-to-do young man about town, complete even to a monocle, seemed destined to remain shut up in that self-satisfied, comfortable little world to which most of the characters in his novels and plays belong.

An aimless social existence did not long appeal to him, however. He travelled adventurously in the Pacific and the Far East, and on the voyage home he met Joseph Conrad, the Polish seaman who became a great English novelist and Galsworthy's lifelong friend. He met other people who un-settled him. He began to discover the dreadful London slums of that time, from some of which his father drew rents, and he was horrified by what he found. The hypocrisy of his own class became intolerable to him. Most disturbing of all he fell deeply in love with his cousin's exceptionally beautiful and tal-ented wife, Ada Galsworthy, who was very unhappy in her marriage. For ten years they maintained a secret love affair, often travelling abroad together. In those days a divorce was a major social sensation and Galsworthy's father would have been deeply distressed by it, so the lovers waited until after his death. They were married in 1905, and John Galsworthy remained devoted to Ada all his life. Some people thought him slavishly devoted.

Because she had been divorced she was shunned by most of their acquaintances, and it was this, coming when he was already deeply unsettled, which finally made Galsworthy rebel against the social class to which he belonged, while it was she who made him into a writer. Although there was no evidence at all except her own intuition, she was absolutely convinced of his latent ability, and reluctant as he was he could not refuse her anything. She helped and encouraged him constantly for the rest of his life. They discussed every detail of his work, and she typed nearly all of it herself, often three times over, for he revised everything meticulously. When he was writing with difficulty nothing helped him so much as her playing to him; she was a fine pianist and they both loved music.

His first book was a volume of feeble and imitative short stories, *From the Four Winds*, published in 1897. This was a failure in every way, and other failures followed, but the tide began to turn with his third novel *The Island Pharisees* (1904); and his fourth, *The Man of Property* (1906) was the first of his chronicles of the Forsyte family. Some people think it is his best work. He published nineteen novels between 1900 and 1933, besides many short stories, but his fame rests mainly on the numerous Forsyte novels and stories, which were collected as *The Forsyte Saga* (1922), *A Modern Comedy* (1929) and *End of the Chapter* (1935), and which achieved such an immense success on television nearly forty years later. Fastidiously written, like all his work, the early Forsyte novels show Galsworthy's shrewd observation of the class against which he had rebelled, the rich merchants who then governed Britain and who were sometimes so possessed by their love of money and property that as human beings they were destroyed by it. But the later novels, in which he arraigned the young people of the nineteen-twenties, sentimentalized the older Forsytes into much less unsympathetic figures. In fact the youthful rebel became the elderly conservative, as rebels so often do, but not before his writings and personal influence had contributed valuably to the movement towards greater social justice.

The novels show also his compassionate sympathy for the poor and oppressed, although he never understood them as well as he understood the rich. It is a powerful sympathy, which shows most clearly in his plays, many of which, from *The Silver Box* (1906) onwards, are clearly the work of a social reformer. He wrote twenty full-length plays and a number of short ones, and published also numerous volumes of verse, essays and lectures.

As his fame and popularity grew he mellowed into the eminent and widely respected man of letters. He and his wife were well received everywhere. He refused a knighthood, but accepted a distinguished British honour, the Order of Merit, in 1929, and honorary doctorates from many universities. He was awarded the Nobel Prize for Literature in 1932, and characteristically he gave the prize money to the P.E.N., the international fellowship of writers of which he was the first President. It still flourishes, and its objects are still those so dear to Galsworthy's heart: "to promote the friendly co-operation of writers in every country in the interests of literature, freedom of expression and international goodwill."

Apart from an interlude of hospital work, with his wife, during the First World War (and he loathed war), Galsworthy lived the quiet life of a successful man of letters who loved dogs and horses and worked hard. He usually gave away half his income, and he lived on a modest scale in London, Devonshire and elsewhere, but he and Ada travelled very widely about the world, mainly at her instigation. His large and continuous literary output and his travels would have been more than enough for most men, but all through his working life he gave much of his time to social and political causes, among them slum clearance, a minimum wage for workers in "sweated" industries, reforms in the divorce law and the prison system, votes for women, improvements in slaughter houses, and better working conditions for ponies in mines. The help which he gave privately to innumerable people in need was never publicized.

He died at Grove Lodge, Hampstead, in north London, on January 31st, 1933.

STRIFE

AND GALSWORTHY THE DRAMATIST

Strife was the third of Galsworthy's plays, written in 1907 but not performed until 1909, partly because his second play, *Joy*, had been a failure when produced in London in 1907. But his first play, *The Silver Box*, which was much more characteristic of him than *Joy* was, had attracted a good deal of attention, and *Strife* was written in the same manner.

The Silver Box was produced in 1906 at the Court Theatre, London, which was making theatrical history then, just as, fifty years later, it made history again with John Osborne's *Look Back in Anger*. The series of plays produced at the Court Theatre from 1904 to 1907, and brilliantly directed by J. E. Vedrenne and Harley Granville-Barker, was a landmark: it included new plays by Shaw, Yeats, Granville-Barker, Gilbert Murray, Masefield, Galsworthy and others, and it began the modern era of English drama.

This theatrical revolution was not limited to Britain, however; it was European, and the two great leaders were the Norwegian, Henrik Ibsen (1828–1906), whose plays were translated into many languages, including English, and the Irishman, George Bernard Shaw (1856–1950), writing in English, whose plays also were widely translated. John Galsworthy followed with a distinctively English, although less substantial contribution. His plays too were presently translated and performed in other countries.

The Silver Box showed that a new dramatist had appeared, with a style and attitude of his own. His aim, as he said later himself, was "to create such an illusion of actual life passing on the stage as to compel the spectator to pass through an experience of his own, to think and talk and move with the people he sees thinking and talking and moving in front of him." Moreover Galsworthy gave the audience something important to think and talk about, a social problem or a question of conscience. *The Silver Box* was in fact a "play of ideas," and although it did not draw large audiences, it was the most discussed play of the year.

So many such "plays of ideas" have been written since that we take them for granted, but in 1906 they were revolutionary, and often resented, for audiences of those days had long been accustomed to artificial plays written solely for light entertainment, with little artistic quality. The new drama was not well received at first by theatregoers, but Galsworthy (and others) went on writing serious plays, among his most notable, besides *The Silver Box*, being *Strife* (1909), *Justice* (1910), *Loyalties* (1922) and *Escape* (1926).

It was through his plays rather than his novels that Galsworthy exercised his strongest influence for social reforms, but since he was always more artist than reformer he was sometimes aggrieved if his plays were valued more highly as propaganda than as drama. A decade later he wrote, perhaps rather inconsistently, in the collected edition of his works: "A dramatist [he means himself] strongly and pitifully impressed by the encircling pressure of modern environments . . . will not write plays detached from the movements and problems of his times. He is not conscious, however, of any desire to solve those problems in his plays or to effect great reforms. His only ambition in drama, as in his other work, is to present truth as he sees it and, gripping with it his readers or his audience, to produce in them a sort of mental and moral ferment, whereby vision may be enlarged, imagination livened and understanding promoted."

Although *Strife* was written so early in his long career as a dramatist, many people have considered it to be his best play. He wrote it in a few months, at various places in southern England, but revised and revised it with the meticulous care which he gave to all his work. As usual he sent the manuscript to friends for comment, particularly Edward Garnett, a well-known writer and critic, and the great novelist, Joseph Conrad. The former suggested some improvements; the latter prophesied that it would more than counteract the failure of *Joy* and would be received with acclamation, as indeed it was. Several theatre-managers refused it, however, and it was not until after it had been produced with some success in Manchester, in the north of England, that a London manager, Charles Frohmann, took the risk of putting it on at the Duke of York's Theatre on March 9th, 1909. It was to be given only six matinee performances, but it was so well received that it was transferred to the Haymarket and then the Adelphi Theatre, to run in the evenings. It attracted even more attention and discussion than *The Silver Box*. Many press notices appeared.* "Not often have we witnessed more genuine enthusiasm in a threatre than was accorded to Mr. Galsworthy's *Strife*," said *The Globe* of the first performance. A leading drama critic, William Archer, put at the head of his long notice, "Mr. Galsworthy arrives," and in *Punch* the heading was "A Great Play." There were of course some unfavourable comments; *The Daily Graphic* complained that it was "an argument rather than an entertainment" and not for "everybody's money," but *The Times* amply offset them all: "If we are not mistaken, when an artist of Mr. Galsworthy's high endeavour, mental equipment and technical skill writes a play like *Strife*, he has done much more than write a play, he has rendered a public service."

This must have given John Galsworthy particular pleasure, for much of his life was given to rendering public services, but he disclaimed any suggestion that *Strife* was written as propaganda. There was much destructive bitterness in industrial relations then, as at many other times, and to this extent the play was highly topical, but he said that he simply used the strike to provide material for his theme: the waste and tragedy which come when fanatics clash. Some people found *Strife* prejudiced, others found it cold-bloodedly detached. He himself wrote with evident amusement, in 1931: "I remember that after a production of *Strife* at Nottingham a

---

* They are quoted here from *The Life and Letters of John Galsworthy*, by H. V. Marrot and *The Man of Principle: A view of John Galsworthy*, by Dudley Barker, to both of which the editor gratefully acknowledges his indebtedness.

certain capitalist came up to me and said, 'By Jove, sir, I did enjoy that speech you gave to old Anthony; that's the stuff to give them', or words to that effect. He was a genial soul and I trust that the expression of my face did not shatter his illusions, I remember that the same year, after a production of *Strife* at Oxford, a Labour 'fan' came up to see me on the platform as I was going back to town and said: 'Ah! that speech of Roberts was great; it got the blighters plumb centre!' or words to *that* effect. He was an engaging enthusiast and again I trust that the look in my eye did not destroy his faith. . . . People shouldn't go to *Strife* [to see Capital or Labour beaten, or] to see a photographic reproduction of an industrial struggle. . . . They should go to *Strife* to see human nature in the thick of a fight, the 'heroism' of diehardism, and the nemesis that dogs it. That is what the author meant them to see in *Strife* when he wrote it. . . ."

Authors are not invariably right about their own work, since it means something to them which it cannot mean to anyone else. So it is for the reader or spectator of today to make up his own mind about *Strife* and to decide, in particular, whether it is a revelation of human nature, a study of social and personal problems, which is of permanent interest and value.

HOW FAR HAVE WE UNDERSTOOD?

QUESTIONS FOR DISCUSSION AND COMPOSITION

Act I

1. A play often begins with some unimportant conversation. Why is this? When does the action of this play really begin?
2. Why does Anthony refer to "the kettle and the pot"?
3. What were the causes of the strike?
4. Why is Harness's accent slightly nasal? What do we learn about him from this act?
5. What arguments does Anthony use in support of his attitude, and how convincing are they?
6. Which of the characters try to persuade Anthony to compromise, and what are the arguments they use?
7. What humour, if any, is there in this act?
8. What are the differences in character and attitude between the various directors?

Act II

9. Write a short account of the discussion between Mrs. Roberts and Enid and say what you think about it.
10. Was Mrs. Roberts justified in refusing help from Enid?
11. What does Jan's part contribute to the play?
12. Have you found any clumsiness in the construction of this act?
13. How much money has Roberts given to support the strike? How did he get it? What bearing has this on the situation and what does it tell us about Roberts?
14. Compare Harness and Rous with Roberts.
15. What is Roberts's opinion of the other strikers and how far is it borne out by their behaviour?

16. Make lists of the men who support Roberts and those who oppose him, giving their reasons.

17. What decision is reached at the strikers' meeting, and for what reasons?

18. How far is it true to say that Roberts was responsible for his wife's death?

Act III

19. How do Anthony and his son Edgar differ in this act?

20. "When I went," says Enid, "I was all on their side, but as soon as I got there I began to feel quite different at once." Why did she change?

21. What are Frost's views of Anthony and of the situation?

22. What are Enid's feelings when Madge Thomas approaches the child's frock?

23. "Ye would never sign them terms! . . . I reckoned on ye!" Why is this one of the most significant speeches in the play?

24. What was the difference between the terms agreed upon and the terms which Roberts wanted?

25. Write a short account of the ending of the strike which might have appeared in the *Trenartha News*.

26. In a preface which he wrote for the plays, about 1923, in the Manaton Edition, the collected edition of his works, John Galsworthy said: "The English man and woman of today do not express themselves glowingly, they have almost a genius for under-expression, and even on the stage seem to resent being made to 'slop over'. . . . I may find this severe technique good, not only for the dramatist, who is cleansed by a sort of self-inflicted purgatory, but for the audience, who, not getting the passions torn to tatters* for them, must use their imaginations more freely to obtain a full effect. . . . The best moment in any of my plays is perhaps that when Anthony

---

* This is an echo of Hamlet's famous speech about acting: "O, it offends me to the soul, to hear a robustious periwig-pated fellow tear a passion to tatters, to very rags . . ." (Part of a long speech in *Hamlet*, Act III, Scene II.)

and Roberts bow humbly to each other in mutual defeat. An Irishman or a poet must have given them a page each."

Do you think the play would have ended more powerfully if Anthony and Roberts had spoken at length about their defeat? Give the arguments on both sides.

27. Can you find any passages in the play which show "almost a genius for understatement"? Does any character ever "slop over"?

GENERAL

28. Why is a play like this described as naturalistic or realistic? How does it differ from a poetic play such as one of Shakespeare's?

29. Are any of the stage directions intended for the reader, not for the player or producer?

30. Which of the stage-directions should be most helpful to the player or the producer?

31. In the theatre of Shakespeare's time, as in some others, there was little or no scenery and the action could therefore move from one place to another, with no break, any number of times. But in a play with realistic stage settings, such as one of Galsworthy's, the number of scene changes must be limited, and this makes the construction of the play more difficult for the playwright. Can you find signs of such difficulties in *Strife*?

32. Where does the climax of the play, the point of highest tension, occur, and how is the tension released?

33. In Act I Wilder says that Wanklin has "Radical views." What evidence of this can you find in the play?

34. What is Enid's part in the play? What would it lose if she were not in it?

35. Write a short letter from Scantlebury to a friend of his, telling the story of the strike and the settlement. You must first of all get to understand his character and his point of view.

36. Who is the most reasonable, fair-minded man in the play, and how does he show it?

37. Are Anthony and Roberts misrepresented in any way by what their friends and enemies say about them?

38. Compare and contrast Anthony and Roberts.

39. At which point, if any, are you sorry for Anthony, and why?

40. Describe the character of Madge Thomas and the part she plays.

41. Which of the characters do you like and dislike most, and why? If you were acting in the play which part would you most like to take, and why?

42. When and by whom were the following said? Explain the full significance of the words:

(*a*) I can't go back on Roberts.

(*b*) It isn't personal, it's the Dad.

(*c*) My wife's ill!

(*d*) You think that with your gloved hands you can cure the trouble of a century.

(*e*) That may suit you but it doesn't suit me, or anyone else I should think.

(*f*) Lucky it's her mother—not her children—you have to look after.

(*g*) You know what it'll all end in.

(*h*) You've dug a pit for yourselves.

(*i*) I'm a humane man—we're all humane men.

(*j*) Have some champagne with your lunch, Mr. Harness.

(*k*) Have to eat another dinner at that hotel.

43. Was this mainly a struggle between "Capital" and "Labour" or between Anthony and Roberts?

44. Is Galsworthy impartial or does he take sides?

45. Arrange a debate on the motion "That in the opinion of this house Mr. Anthony was in the wrong." This needs careful preparation. The speakers, in this order, should be (1) the proposer of the motion; (2) the opposer; (3) the seconder of the motion; (4) the opposer's seconder. The chairman then declares the debate open for anyone present in

the "house" to speak, but no one may speak more than once except that, at the end, speakers (2) and (1) speak again, in that order, to deal with any important points which have been raised. It is essential to have a strong, impartial chairman, who takes no part in the debate, maintains order, calls upon each speaker in turn and sees that no speaker goes beyond an agreed time-limit, say ten minutes each for (1) and (2) and five minutes for each of the others. At the very end he takes a vote on the motion, by show of hands or by ballot papers, and announces the result.

46. It has been said that the only villain in this play is the social order of that time. Do you agree?

47. What is the theme, the central idea, of the play and what is the moral?

48. Compare *Strife* with any great tragedy which you know. Do you regard *Strife* as a great tragedy?

ACTING NOTES

A PLAY is written to be performed, and the printed text, like a musical score, is simply the basis for a performance. When reading to himself the reader should hear and see everything, and the practised, imaginative reader can stage a good performance in his own mind; but drama is a communal art, and it is only as a combination of sound, movement and pictorial effect, presented to an audience, that a play can come fully to life.

Any group of people studying this play for their own purposes should attempt at least a half-performance, walking about book in hand, and rehearsing some if not all of the scenes by reading them several times and trying to make improvements every time. If the group wish to please an audience they should not choose this play for performance unless they can cast it fairly well, and in particular they must have players who can give acceptable renderings of Anthony and Roberts.

The group must also have a producer whose rulings they will accept and who will take charge of the production in much the same way as a conductor takes charge of an orchestra. The producer is responsible for the artistic harmony and unity of the play in all its details, and the success of the performance will depend largely on his knowledge, imagination, tact, enthusiasm, and willingness to learn.

When the play has been chosen, application for permission to perform it should be made *at once* to The Secretary, The Incorporated Society of Authors, 84 Drayton Gardens, London S.W.10, giving the name of the amateur company and the number, place and dates of the performances they wish to give.

The other business arrangements should also be started well in advance, booking the hall, finding printers for posters, tickets and programmes, getting lighting equipment, stage

settings and so on. A detailed list of everything which has to be
done should be made at a very early stage, and responsibilities
should be allocated in writing.

Several auditions—trial readings—may be necessary before
all the parts are finally cast, and before rehearsals can begin
the producer must study the play very thoroughly, with his
cast and stage in mind. He must see and hear clearly everything which happens. He should make himself a prompt-book,
by breaking up two copies of the play and sticking the leaves
on alternate pages of an exercise book. This gives him space
for a stage-plan, or a series of stage-plans, for every scene,
showing the position of furniture, doors, etc., and the entrances,
movements, groupings, exits, etc., of the players, with notes
on lighting, "noises off," etc. Since the play is the work of a
very skilful and experienced playwright the author's stage-
directions should be followed if they suit the stage to be used
and the producer's interpretation of the play.

Every player should have a copy of the play for himself, so
that he can study it as a whole, but he should not begin learning
his part by heart until after the first rehearsals have been held
and he has been shown his entrances, exits, and most important movements, so that he can associate these with words
from the start. He must then learn his part, and cues, as
quickly as possible. If the rehearsals are not held on the stage,
a plan of the stage must be marked out on the floor of the
rehearsal room; otherwise the change to the stage may confuse
movements and groupings very badly.

Strife is obviously a realistic play which would gain from
realistic settings, and these are not numerous or difficult. The
play can, however, be given quite successfully in a curtain
setting. This is much better than unconvincing attempts at
realism and long waits for scene-changing, which do great
damage to a performance. It would be an advantage, but is
not essential, to have two sets of curtains; one very shabby,
or very dull, set for the Roberts's kitchen and for the strikers'
meeting, and the other set, dark blue or green or brown, for
the Underwoods' dining-room and drawing-room. The same

setting, or almost the same, can be used for these two rooms.

Lighting is always important, but *Strife* gives little scope for subtlety or variation. The depression of Act II, Scene I, should be accentuated by dimmer lighting, and the failing light of Act II, Scene II, must also be suggested, but (as in all scenes) it must be bright enough for faces to be seen clearly from the back of the hall. Headlights and footlights must be adjusted to eliminate unwanted shadows.

In *Strife*, as in most plays, scene-changing and lighting rehearsals are essential if mistakes, delays and noise are to be avoided.

Costumes of 1909 are almost essential; Edwardian England belongs to the past as surely as Victorian England. In particular the strikers must be a great deal shabbier than they would be today. At least the attempt to suggest the costumes should be made. Any good library may have magazines of the time, such as *The Illustrated London News* and *Punch*, and there are numerous illustrated histories and biographies covering the period.

But it is the acting which makes or ruins the performance. The players are very unlikely to be great actors but they can learn in rehearsal some of the rudiments of good acting. They must be word-perfect in their parts. (There should be, however, a reliable prompter in a strategic position during the last few rehearsals and during the performances.) Every word must be clearly audible at the back of the hall—which is secured by clear articulation, not by shouting. Cues must be taken promtly. (Slowness in taking cues is one of the commonest and most fatal defects of amateur acting.) Every player must know and understand the play as a whole, and must act every minute he is on the stage, no matter how small his part may be. When he has nothing to say or do he must continue to be the character he represents; he must react, although not always visibly, to everything which happens, remembering always that this character never knows what is going to happen next; it is only the player who knows that.

It is for the producer to give every scene a dramatic shape.